**VICTORIAN HATS
VOL. 4 – 1890-1899**

Compiled and Edited by
Millicent René

Copyright© 2007 Ageless Patterns™

This edition contains re-typed articles and illustrations from *Harper's Bazar* 1890-1899

All rights reserved. No part of this work may be reproduced without permission.

ISBN 0-9723189-8-4
Library of Congress Control Number: 2006903319

Printed in the United States of America

Published by:
Ageless Patterns
PO Box 6118
Chino Valley, AZ 86323 USA

FORWARD

This book contains 221 illustrations complete with descriptions from *Harper's Bazar* magazines faithfully re-typed for legibility. It is meant to be a guide for costumers, milliners and for those who love to sew Victorian clothing during the period of 1890 and 1899.

Dedicated to all who love to sew!!

By Millicent René

Victorian Hair-do's & Coiffures
1867-1898

Victorian Hats
Vol. 4 – 1890-1899

Victorian Hats
Vol. 3 – 1880-1889

Victorian Masquerade Costumes
1867-1898

Victorian Hats
Vol. 2 – 1870-1879

Victorian Hats
Vol. 1 – 1867-1869

Harper's Bazar Cut Paper Patterns
Vol. 1 – 1870-1879

Men's Victorian Fashions
1867-1899

Victorian Parasols
1867-1899

How To Sew Harper's Bazar
1867-1898

VICTORIAN HATS
VOL. 4 - 1890-1899

April 19, 1890
SPRING BONNETS

The spring-like little bonnet has a flat crown only of open lace straw banded with black velvet ribbon, a pointed diadem of yellow primroses taking the place of a brim. Some black lace is draped irregularly toward one side and secured with a jet clasp, and narrow lace scarfs are drawn forward from the middle of the back, where they are attached, and tied loosely under the chin.

April 19, 1890
SPRING BONNETS

Another bonnet shown is of black lace with pink. The brim of this is wider and flaring, with the edge softened by wide drooping lace; the lace is drawn in folds along the sides, its ends forming the strings. The shirred lace crown is framed in a horseshoe-shaped ornament of jet with pendants. A pink ribbon band and bow and bunches of pink blossoms are the trimming.

April 19, 1890
SPRING BONNETS

The wide-brimmed black lace round hat has a long-stemmed bunch of roses and honeysuckle tied to one side, with a black velvet ribbon bow, and strings of narrower velvet ribbon.

May 31, 1890
SUMMER HATS

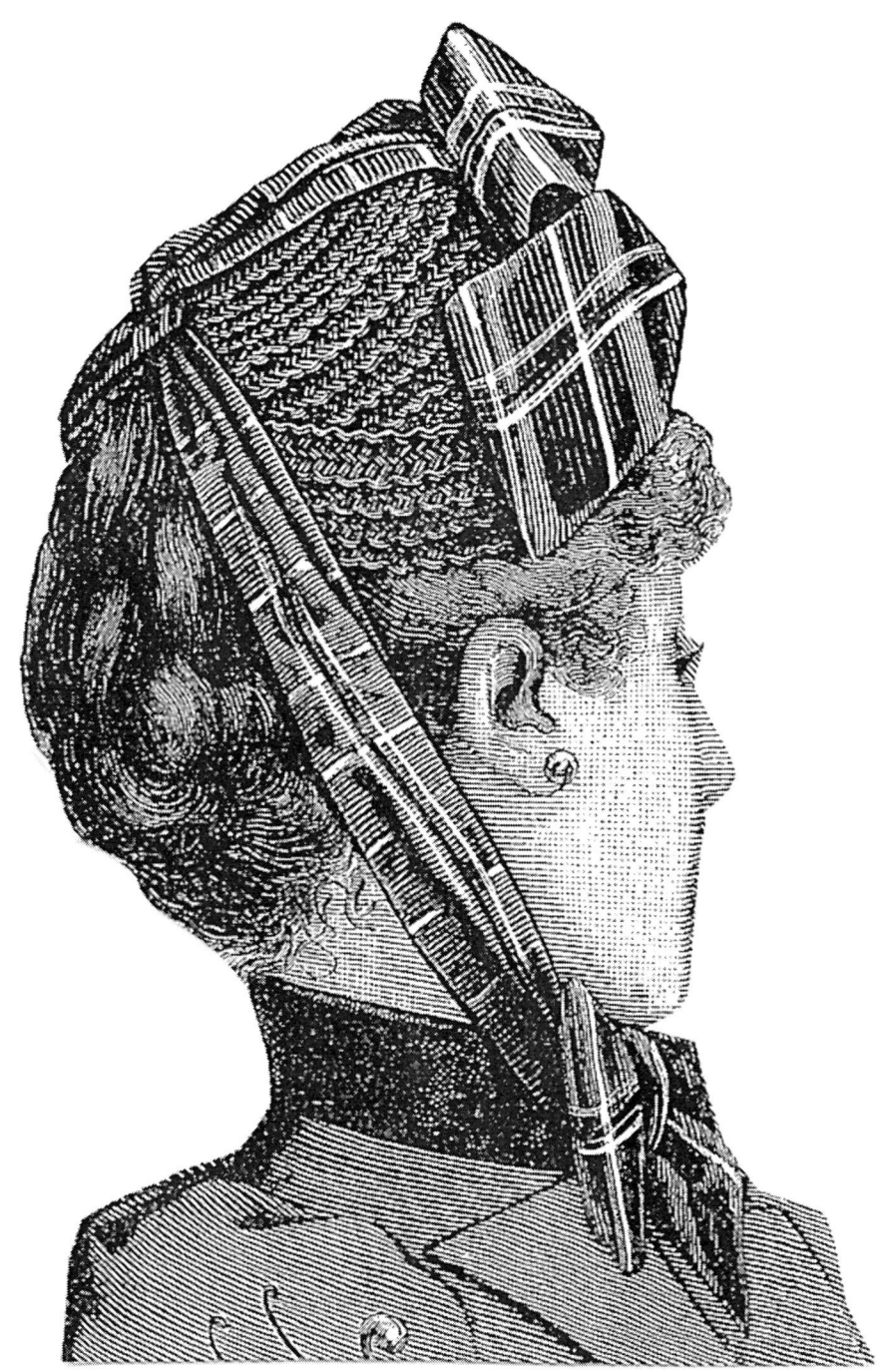

A bonnet for a morning or traveling toilette is of navy blue rough straw, trimmed with plaid ribbon. The ribbon is formed into an Alsacian bow on the front, then carried down the middle of the crown and crossed at the back, the ends being brought forward for strings.

May 31, 1890
SUMMER HATS

A wide round hat, with a brim which is turned up and slashed at the back, is of black chip, with an open border inserted in the brim. It is faced with black tulle. The garniture is a scarf of white tulle with an embroidered edge, which is draped about the crown, and to which a cluster of five white ostrich tips is added.

May 31, 1890
SUMMER HATS

The flat black lace hat illustrated has an open-top crown surrounded with a wreath of pink roses held by a jet band. The bows and strings are of narrow Jacqueminot red velvet ribbon.

November 1, 1890
WINTER HATS AND BONNETS

The young lady's bolero turban is of gray felt, with a half-inch fold of black velvet bordering the brim and two similar folds encircling the crown and terminating in small bows on the side. Two large variegated feather pompons form the trimming.

November 1, 1890
WINTER HATS AND BONNETS

A prune-colored velvet bonnet shown has a shallow crown on which the velvet is drawn together at the center. The brim is double, the outer layer narrower that the inner, both being covered with dark velvet, and faced with anemone-colored velvet which shows in a narrow binding at the edge. Anemone-colored ribbon is folded around the crown and tied with strings of the dark velvet at the back, while at the front it is looped under both brims and a cluster of ostrich tips of the same color is added.

November 1, 1890
WINTER HATS AND BONNETS

A platinum gray velvet bonnet is in "tortoise-shape", with a separate brim set inside. Thirteen small shaded gray ostrich tips frame the front. A twisted band of gray velvet rims the back. The strings are light gray ribbon.

November 1, 1890
WINTER HATS

A silver gray felt hat of the wide-brimmed *capeline* variety is shown. The brim is narrower and turned up at the back. The crown is draped with darker platinum gray velvet, ornamented with a silver clasp at the front. A group of three white ostrich feathers is massed at the back, one of them drooping over the back of the brim.

**November 1, 1890
WINTER HATS**

A wide-brimmed black velvet hat, peaked at the front. The crown consists of a drooping puff of black velvet, which is encircled by a band of olive green velvet, tied in a long bow at the front; a similar bow is at the back. Six black ostrich tips are grouped on the crown, drooping to front and back.

November 1, 1890
WINTER HATS

A black and orange bonnet shown in the illustration has the brim of orange velvet veiled with black lace, and the crown composed of three puffs of black velvet, banded with orange bands on which narrow black ostrich trimming is set. A group of four ostrich feathers is at the back, and toward the right side a black and an orange pompon with an aigrette. Strings of narrow black velvet ribbon.

November 1, 1890
WINTER HATS

The wide beaver hat illustrated is golden brown in color. A lace barbe is arranged in loops and ends on the front, and some similar lace is on the back, with the ends stiffened with wire. Two black birds nestle at the front.

November 22, 1890
PARIS HATS

YOUNG LADY'S HAT – This novel hat for a young lady is of gray braided felt, with its wide brim jauntily turned back in front, and held against the crown by a broad strap of gray faille ribbon. Loops of ribbon cover the crown, and hold some long-stemmed velvet iris flowers. Tulle skeleton-leaf feathers are thrust in the ribbon.

**November 22, 1890
PARIS HATS**

THEATRE BONNET – A theatre bonnet of original design represents a butterfly. It is made of three fans of tulle, two turned flatly toward the face, the third erect at the back. Two tulle feathers stand erect as wings. It may be entirely of black tulle, and is very effective when of black and gold. The veil is fastened by two jet butterflies.

**November 22, 1890
WINTER HATS**

A black felt hat is illustrated, the crown of which is of smooth French felt, while the brim is shaggy beaver felt. Black and red variegated ostrich feathers form the trimming, comprising one long plume and a group of shorter tips. Black velvet ribbon strings come from the back, encircle the throat, and tie at the side.

November 22, 1890
WINTER HATS

A low-crowned shaggy seal brown beaver felt has for its sole ornament a gleaming paroquet, with long tail feathers drooping at the back.

November 22, 1890
WINTER HATS

A silver gray felt hat is trimmed with white lace, which is frilled on the brim, and surmounted by bows of white ribbon, the back of the wide brim being also caught up by a white bow.

**November 22, 1890
WINTER HATS**

A boat-shaped heliotrope felt hat is draped with a black net scarf, the scalloped edge of which rests on the edge of the brim. Black velvet ribbon bows, and black feather pompons trim the back, and a bunch of violets rests on the front of the brim.

December 6, 1890
WINTER HATS

YOUNG LADY'S HAT – A black felt hat for a young lady has the crown draped with violet velvet, which is irregularly puffed, drawn up in points toward the front and carried under the brim at the back. Clusters of light and dark rhododendrons are fastened one at the front and the other at the back underneath the brim.

December 6, 1890
WINTER HATS

YOUNG LADY'S HAT – A tan-colored felt hat, with smooth crown and brim of beaver felt, is shown. A scarf of emerald velvet is twined about the crown, and a fancy feather composed of green wings with an aigrette ornaments the front.

**December 6, 1890
WINTER HATS**

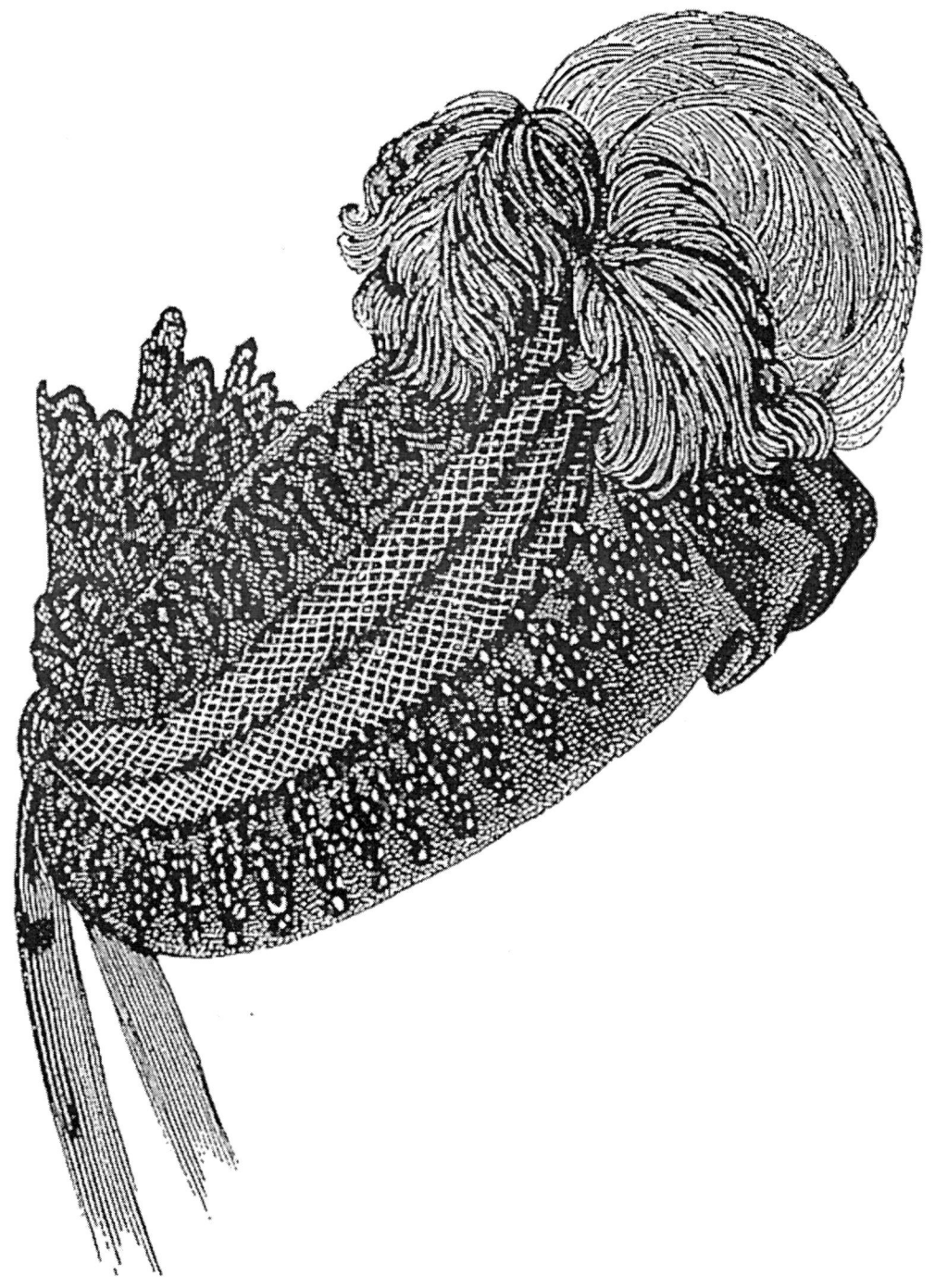

VELVET BONNET – Is a green velvet bonnet, which is ornamented with a jet band on the revers brim. A lace-edged not scarf is draped about the crown, and arranged in fan pleats at the back, where narrow black velvet strings are added.

**December 6, 1890
WINTER HATS**

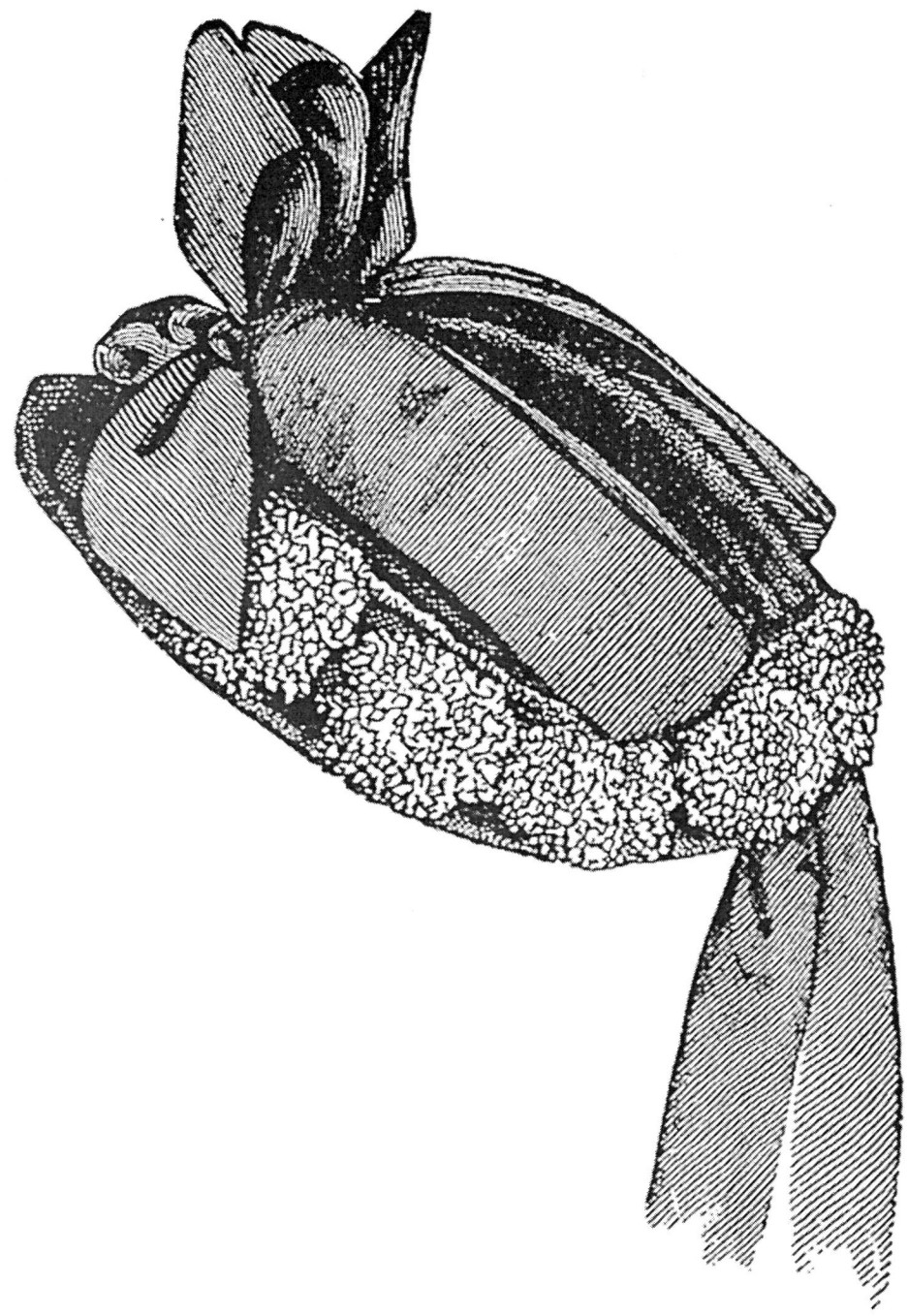

VELVET BONNET – A purple velvet capote is surrounded with a glittering band of passementerie of steel beads, spangles, and threads. An *aubergine* ribbon is tied in a bow on the front, and brought along the sides to terminate in strings at the back.

January 10, 1891
PARIS HATS

WIDE-BRIMMED VELVET HAT – A youthful round hat with soft crown and projecting brim is of *marron* velvet trimmed with ostrich feathers of the same shade, and high loops of satin ribbon at the back.

January 10, 1891
PARIS HATS

EVENING CAPOTE – The chapeau Adiny is a dressy evening bonnet of maize-colored velvet laid in large folds over the crown, and trimmed with application lace fancifully bordered. A pretty aigrette of dark feathers is set in front, and the strings are of narrow ribbon.

January 10, 1891
PARIS HATS

SEAL-SKIN AND CLOTH TOQUE – A toque for a young lady has a crown of pale rose-colored cloth in long folds surround with a border of seal-skin fur, and trimmed with miniature heads of seals.

January 10, 1891
PARIS HATS

WALKING HAT – The Amazon hat with visor brim is of dark blue cloth bordered with Astrakhan fur. The crown is folded in bold pleats in front, and is banded with yellow velvet ribbon. A group of black and yellow birds are perched on the back.

March 14, 1891

OXFORD HAT FOR A GIRL OF 8-12 YEARS – This charming little shape is susceptible of such variety that it is worthy of a dozen illustrations. It is also the most feasible shape for an amateur to deal wit, for one can easily make it from first to last if one can procure a half yard of ordinary buckram and a bit of bonnet wire.

Diagram 1 gives the exact pattern of the top piece, a flat piece of buckram place upon the top of a piece shaped like diagram 2, and turned up at the back at line A or B.

It may be made smaller by an inch if desired, but this is the size represented in the illustration – fourteen inches the largest measurement. It is to be attached at the center of the lines A-B to the middle of the line A of the piece represented in diagram 2. The two ends of this piece are attached to the piece represented in diagram 1 at the letters C and D, not meeting, as will be seen, at the front.

Both pieces are to be covered with velvet after they are wired all round, and after being covered are then attached to each other as described. A small bow, either decorated with a buckle or made plainly, finishes the front, placed between C and D.

The hat may be of black velvet with silk or ribbon bows of golden brown or blue-gray, of olive velvet with bows of a little lighter shade, or of dark purple with heliotrope bows. The edge of the hat may be finished with a cord of velvet or a braid of one of the innumerable pretty designs to be found in passementerie.

March 14, 1891

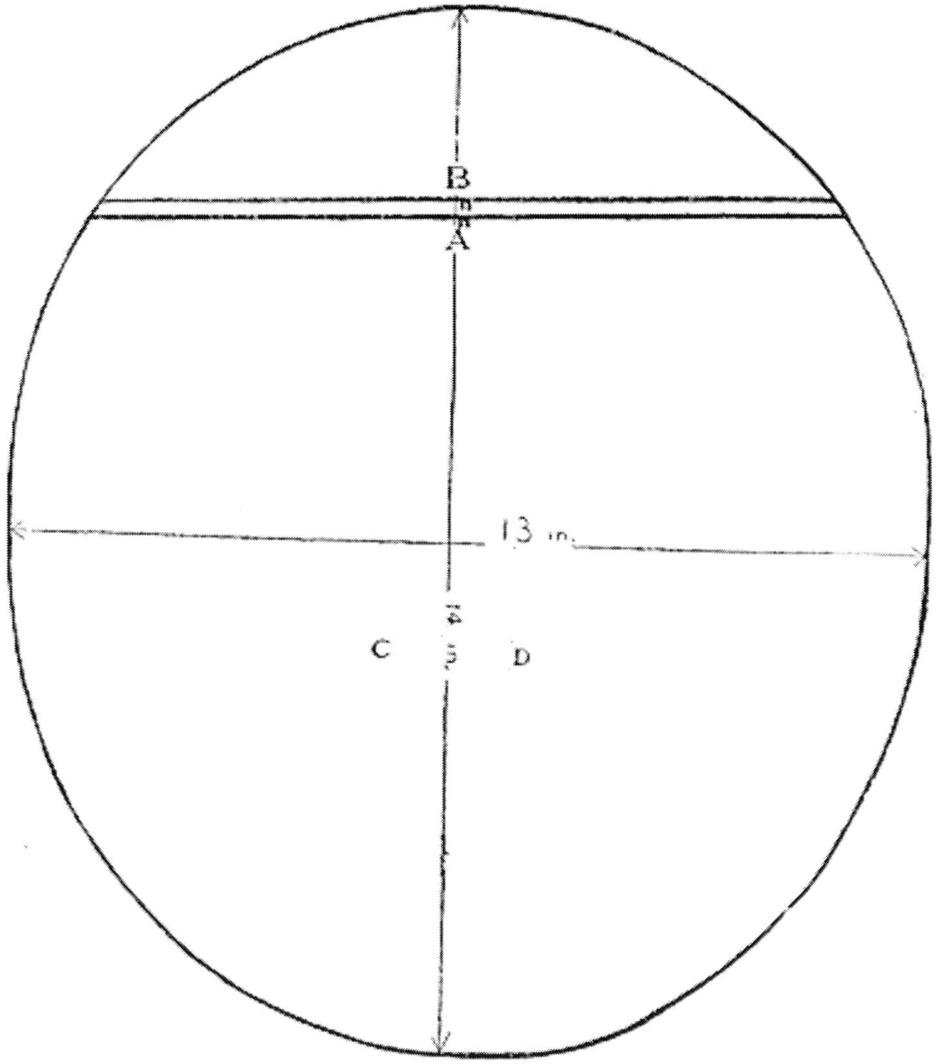

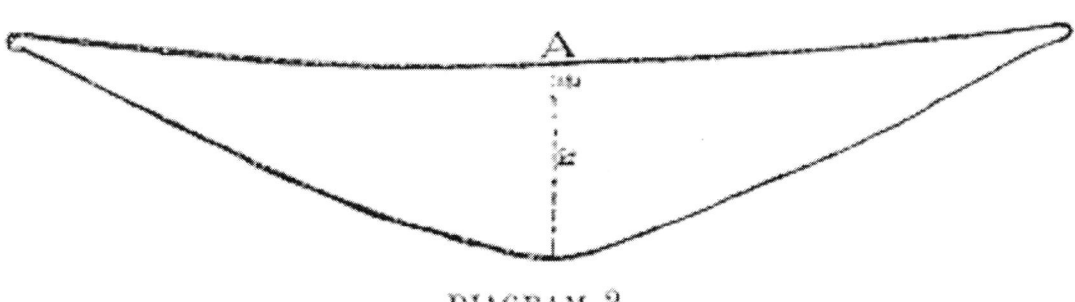

DIAGRAM 1.

DIAGRAM 2.

OXFORD HAT FOR A GIRL OF 8-12 YEARS

March 28, 1891

DEMI-SEASON BONNET – The pretty capote in the illustration is of the wired chenille that will be worn with afternoon toilettes in the demi-season. It has a coronet of chenille, with full loops high in front. Cream white lace with straight edges forms other loops, and surrounds the crown. A black aigrette trims the back.

May 9, 1891

SPRING HAT – This charmingly youthful hat, called Jeune France by the Paris milliners, is a plateau (or flat round) of open fancy straw lined with pink crêpe. A wreath of green violet leaves trims the side, and a pert bow of black velvet is directly in front. A bouquet of long-stemmed Parma violets trims the back. Narrow strings of black velvet.

May 9, 1891

BLACK CHIP HAT WITH ROSES – A wide brimmed hat for summer is of black chip. The brim is turned up at the back, and lined with straw. Changeable yellow and pink satin ribbon is folded around the crown, and tied in a stylish long-looped bow in front. A spray of pink roses falls over the crown and law at the back.

May 9, 1891

BRONZE CIP SUMMER HAT – A pretty hat of bronze-colored chip has its brim strengthened with a straw lining of a similar color. A ruche of green gauze ribbon, narrowly edged with black velvet, surrounds the crown, and is tied in bows in front and back. Bunches of anemones in mauve and yellow shades are held by the bows in front and on the back of the crown.

May 9, 1891

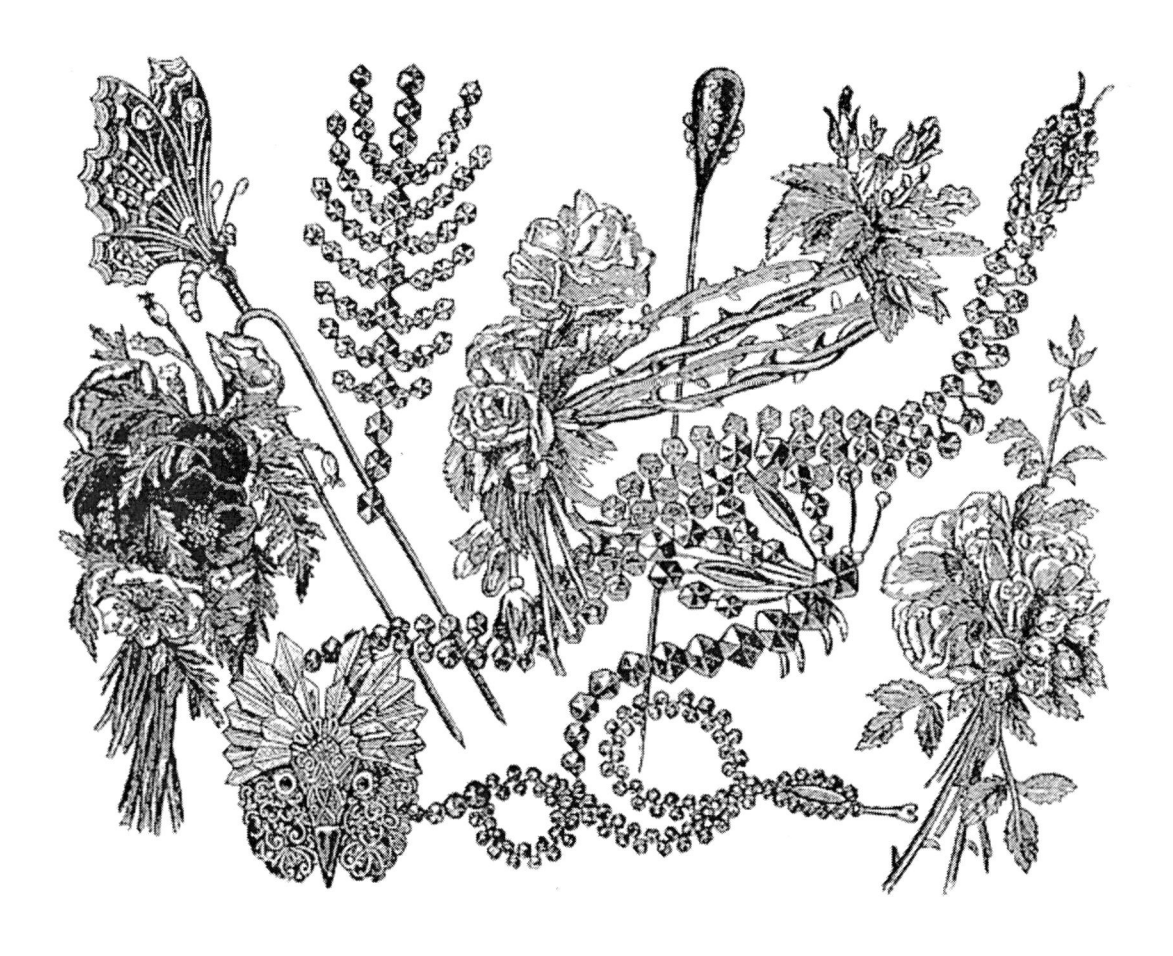

HAT ORNAMENTS – Two of the ornaments illustrated in the group are one of the popular "Cleopatra's asp" variety, the larger, designed for encircling a lace or straw-lace toque, being of cut jet, and the smaller, which is designed for a similar purpose, of iridescent cut steel. A dragon-fly and a skeleton leaf for trimming the front of a small hat are of cut jet. An iridescent metal butterfly quivers on a spiral spring attached to a gilt pin. A wreath, which by the addition of a small quantity of lace and ribbon is converted into a toque, is composed of thorny stems, with a cluster of rose buds and leaves for the front and full-blown roses for the back of the hat. Other flower trimmings represented are a cluster of velvet pansies of variegated colors, and a bunch of pink peonies and buds. The small Egyptian clasp is of oxidized silver and gilt. The hat-pin has a pear-shaped head of mother-of-pearl.

June 20, 1891
SUMMER HATS

Black chip is the material of the wide hat illustrated. The brim is capriciously curved and dented. The trimming is wide plaid surah ribbon, which is arranged in two large irregular bows – one at the front and one at the back of the hat.

June 20, 1891
SUMMER HATS

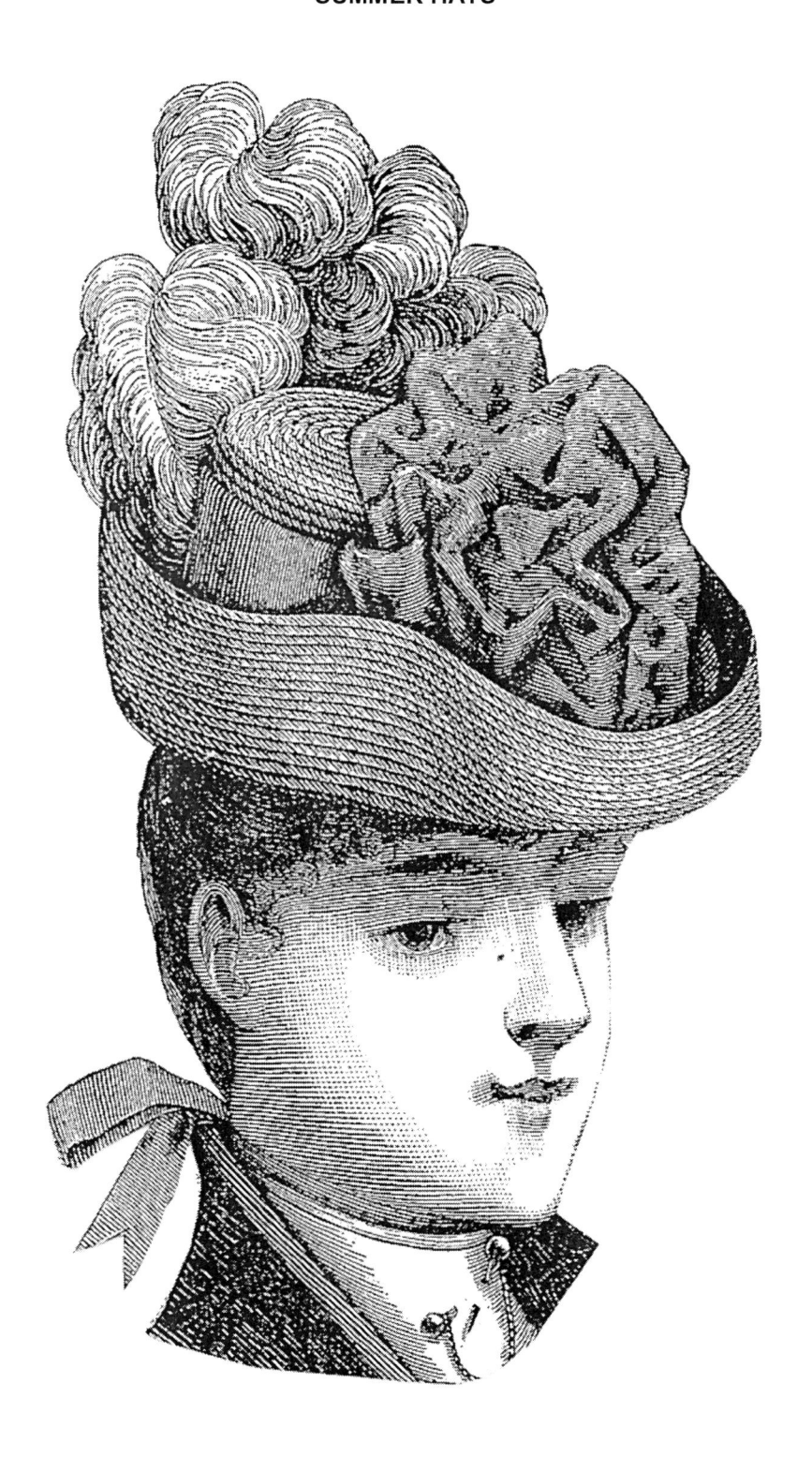

The bolero turban is of gray straw. Gray and rose changeable silk forms a straight band around the crown and a large chou at the front. A cluster of six gray ostrich tips ornaments the back.

June 20, 1891
SUMMER HATS

A traveling or morning bonnet for an elderly lady is of black fancy straw. A bow of four-inch black ribbon trims the front, with folded bands extending down the sides. Strings of black ribbon an inch and a half wide are attached under a bow of the same at the back.

August 8, 1891
SUMMER HATS

CHIP TOQUE – The black chip toque illustrated has a revers brim veiled with a band of cream embroidered chiffon, which is arranged in a bow at the back, surmounted by a bunch of green leaves. The crown is draped in velvet of two shades of green, with a knot of the lighter at the front.

August 8, 1891
SUMMER HATS

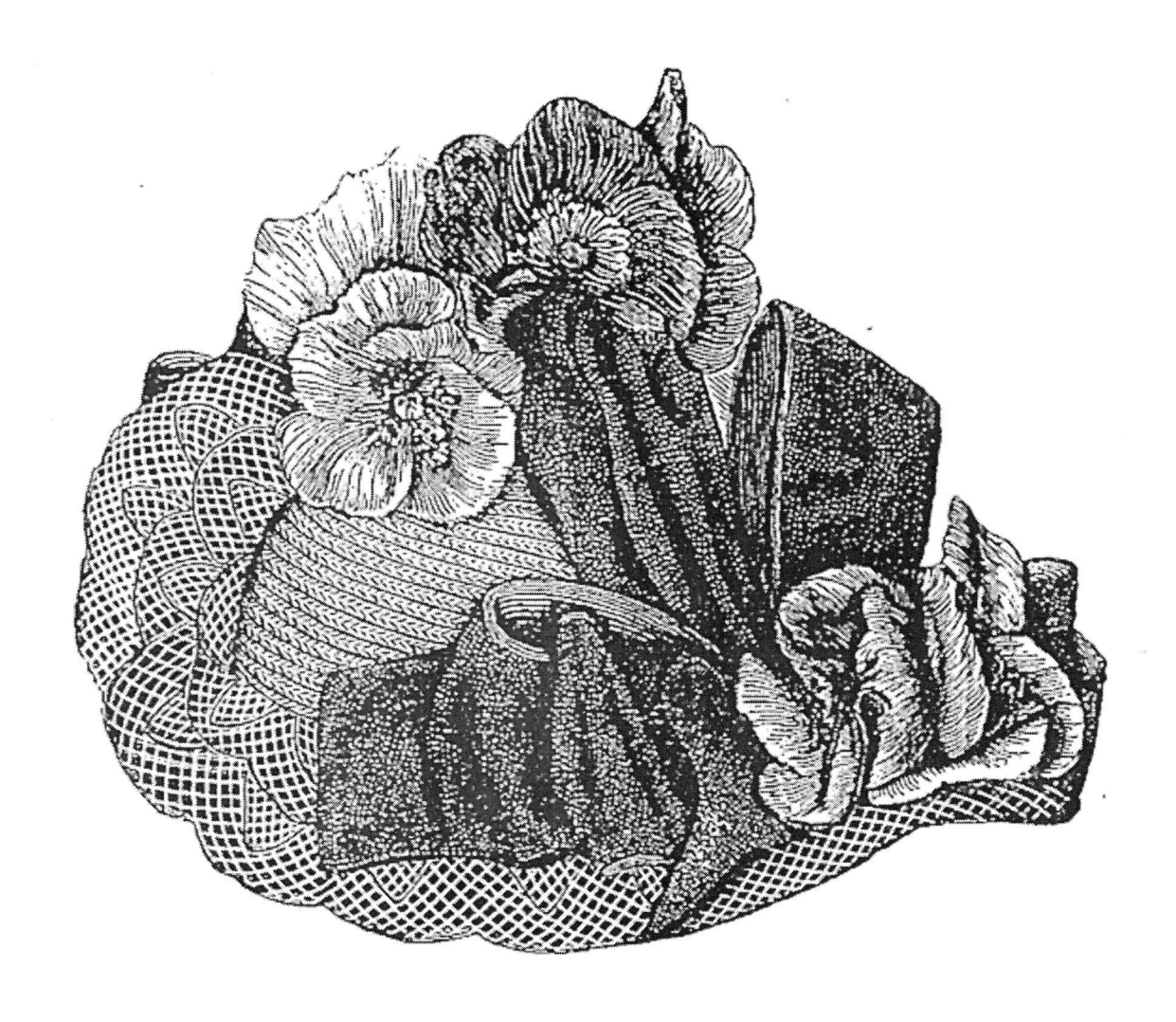

NEAPOLITAN HAT – A white Neapolitan hat with a lace-like brim is trimmed at the front with a large bow of violet velvet ribbon, together with one yellow and one violet blossom. At the back is a larger cluster of similar blossoms held by a bow.

September 19, 1891

DEMI-SEASON BONNET – This capote is composed of three bandeaux covered with black velvet, joined to one another only at the sides. The foremost one is draped with dark red velvet, and ornamented with two long jet wings; a red velvet bow is placed at the middle, caught down with a jet butterfly; a similar smaller bow is on the band at the back, to which the narrow black velvet ribbon strings are attached, and a half-wreath of pink roses is mounted on the middle band.

October 10, 1891

UNTRIMMED AUTUMN AND WINTER FELT HATS – A number of the newest shapes in felt hats for the coming winter are illustrated in this group. They are brought out in all the fashionable shades of gray, green, beige, brown, and navy blue, as well at the inevitable black. The smooth hats shown have a thick silk wide at the edge. One model has an Astrakhan binding, another has an inch deep border composed of alternate rows of silk wire and gold braid, and a third has a wide brim of shaggy ombré felt surrounding the small oval crown of smooth plain colored felt.

November 7, 1891
WINTER HATS AND BONNETS

FELT BOLERO TURBAN - The bolero turban is of black felt, with a deep black ribbon binding on the brim. The sole ornament is a large bow of satin-edged red grosgrain ribbon placed on the left side.

November 7, 1891
WINTER HATS AND BONNETS

A small theatre bonnet of gold-spangle black net is illustrated. The crown of the flat dented net frame is covered with spangle net, and surrounded with a frill of jet and gold lace. Eight small black ostrich tips encircle the crown, drooping over the brim, and an aigrette is placed at the back.

November 7, 1891
WINTER HATS AND BONNETS

A brown velvet round hat is edged with jet cabochons. The crown is surrounded with short upright loops of bronze satin ribbon set on under a velvet fold. A small bow is placed at the middle of the front, and another catches up the brim at the back, within which two black birds are placed.

November 7, 1891
WINTER HATS AND BONNETS

A boat-shaped brown felt hat is trimmed with beige-colored ribbon, which is drawn in two long loops over the crown to the front, with a bow of upright loops at the back; two black quills are at either side of the back.

November 7, 1891
WINTER HATS AND BONNETS

An olive velvet bonnet illustrated has a frame without a crown. The brim is covered on both sides with olive velvet, which on the outside is overlaid with jet trimming. A bias scarf of velvet is gathered in two high puffs to form the full crown, which is encircled by a narrow pink velvet ribbon that is tied in a small bow at the front, and brought down for strings at the back. Two pink ostrich tips trim the back.

November 7, 1891
WINTER HATS AND BONNETS

The very small shell-shaped bonnet shown is of dark green velvet overlaid with jet. Three loops of folded green satin ribbon lie flat on the crown, and a cluster of Nile green ostrich tips is mounted high at the back.

November 7, 1891

VELVET BONNET – This small capote is of red velvet. A row of large cut jet beads finishes the edge. Two shell pins with cut jet beads are thrust crosswise into the velvet. Wired loops and ends of black lace trim the back. The strings are of narrow black velvet ribbon.

November 14, 1891
WINTER HATS

The small bonnet illustrated is made of fawn-colored cloth to match a costume. The cloth is braided with silk soutache to match, and beaded with jet beads, and parts of the wrought design are cut out, showing black velvet laid underneath. A bow of the cloth is at the back, tied with a bow of narrow black velvet ribbon to which the strings are attached, and a light blue aigrette is added. Inside the front is a band with a twist and a small bow of light blue crêpe de Chine.

November 14, 1891
WINTER HATS

A wide-brimmed hat of dark dahlia-colored velvet shown in the illustration is edged with jet, and covered with jet-spangled net on the crown. The brim is draped with wide lace, which at the back is brought up in fan-pleatings to meet a cluster of three black ostrich tips with an aigrette.

November 14, 1891
WINTER HATS

The black felt hat shown has a brim which is dented at the front, turned up at the back, and rolled narrowly at the edge, covering the wire. On the front is an irregularly arranged bow of wide velvet and satin striped ribbon in yellow, violet, and olive, from which rise the points of two black wings. Two other wings are at the back, where the brim is caught up with four folded straps of black ribbon.

April 16, 1892

"RINALDA" HAT FROM VIROT – This "picture" hat, to be worn at Easter-week receptions and throughout the summer, is of black horsehair edged all around with white guipure. Roses without foliage are set closely together under the guipure to hold it up and give it shape. A torsade around the crown and the great bow are of shrimp pink ribbon. Two black feather tips set back to back complete the trimming. Similar hats made of white Neapolitan braid edged with white lace will be worn by bridesmaids at June weddings. The feathers will be white, and the ribbon will match that used in the gowns.

October 1, 1892
WINTER BONNETS AND HATS

A bonnet for an elderly lady is of dark olive velvet. The velvet is drawn in folds on the crown, which are caught together at the bottom of the back with a knot of ribbon with which the strings of lighter olive ribbon are attached. A feather ornament is on the front, supported by a knot of velvet and ribbon loops.
A jaunty black velvet capote with sugar-loaf crown and fluted front has a band of wide gold galloon around the front, caught with jet ornaments in the folds of the velvet, and with knots of folded black faille ribbon at its ends. A group of folded ends of ribbon added to a yellow and black aigrette trims the front.
The "1830" hat is of black velvet, with a flat shirred binding of the same. Folded bands of white and of orange satin ribbon encircle the crown, and form bows, one toward the back on the right side, the other toward the front on the left, where it holds a large white and yellow aigrette. Long streamers of orange ribbon are attached with jet clasps.

October 1, 1892
WINTER BONNETS AND HATS

A dark green felt bonnet is trimmed with violet velvet. A flat Alsacian bow of the velvet is on the front, with two pointed "ears" of velvet rising together with a steel aigrette from a double knot at the middle. The velvet strings are attached with "ears" at the back. A narrow steel band encircles the crown.

A transparent bonnet of black silk passementerie shown in the illustration has a bow of pink velvet ribbon and an aigrette ornamenting the front, and black velvet strings.

A black felt hat is faced with orange velvet under the brim. The trimming comprises a bandeau of black velvet, a large black aigrette tipped with yellow, and loops of yellow ribbon.

October 15, 1892
WINTER HATS

FELT HAT – The felt hat shown is in an odd combination of colors. It is of light beige-colored felt, with a marabout edging of a slightly darker shade. The crown is shallow, with a pointed top, and the brim is sharply dented at the front and bent down at the back. A shirred rim of lilac watered ribbon on wire is set on edge around the crown. Green satin ribbon is added to lilac ribbon to form the bow on the crown, from which ends of green ribbon are carried to front and back, to terminate in a small bow with a jeweled ornament. Two nodding lilac ostrich tips are added to the bow.

October 1, 1892
WINTER BONNETS AND HATS

BEAVER HAT – The wide red beaver hat is trimmed with dark red velvet ribbon. A broad bow of the ribbon held by a steel buckle trims the side of the front, with a tuft of ostrich tips added. A smaller bow catches up the brim at the back.

November 19, 1892

A WINTER HAT – A *plateau* of pink felt forms the crown of this beautiful hat, and is turned up high on the left side and in the back above a brim of black velvet. The raised part on the left is held in place by a tuft of black feathers with an aigrette in the center, beneath which is a pink chrysanthemum of great size. A galloon of black feathers is around the edge, but is visible only on the raised parts of the *plateau*. This graceful design is from Madame Carlier, Avenue de l'Opéra, Paris.

November 19, 1892
WINTER HATS

PLAITED FELT BONNET – The novel little bonnet of which an illustration is given is of plaited brown felt, narrow strips being braided in and out of light blue silk cord, and a galloon of blue and brown silk cords finishes the edges. Three light blue ostrich tips are fastened under a bow of brown velvet ribbon. The strings are of blue ribbon.

November 19, 1892
WINTER HATS

HAT WITH TARTAN TRIMMING – The young lady's round hat is of dark blue felt trimmed with blue, green, and yellow tartan plaid ribbon, and with dark blue plumes changing into green.

March 11, 1893

A SPRING BONNET

March 25, 1893
GIRLS' UNTRIMMED SUMMER HATS

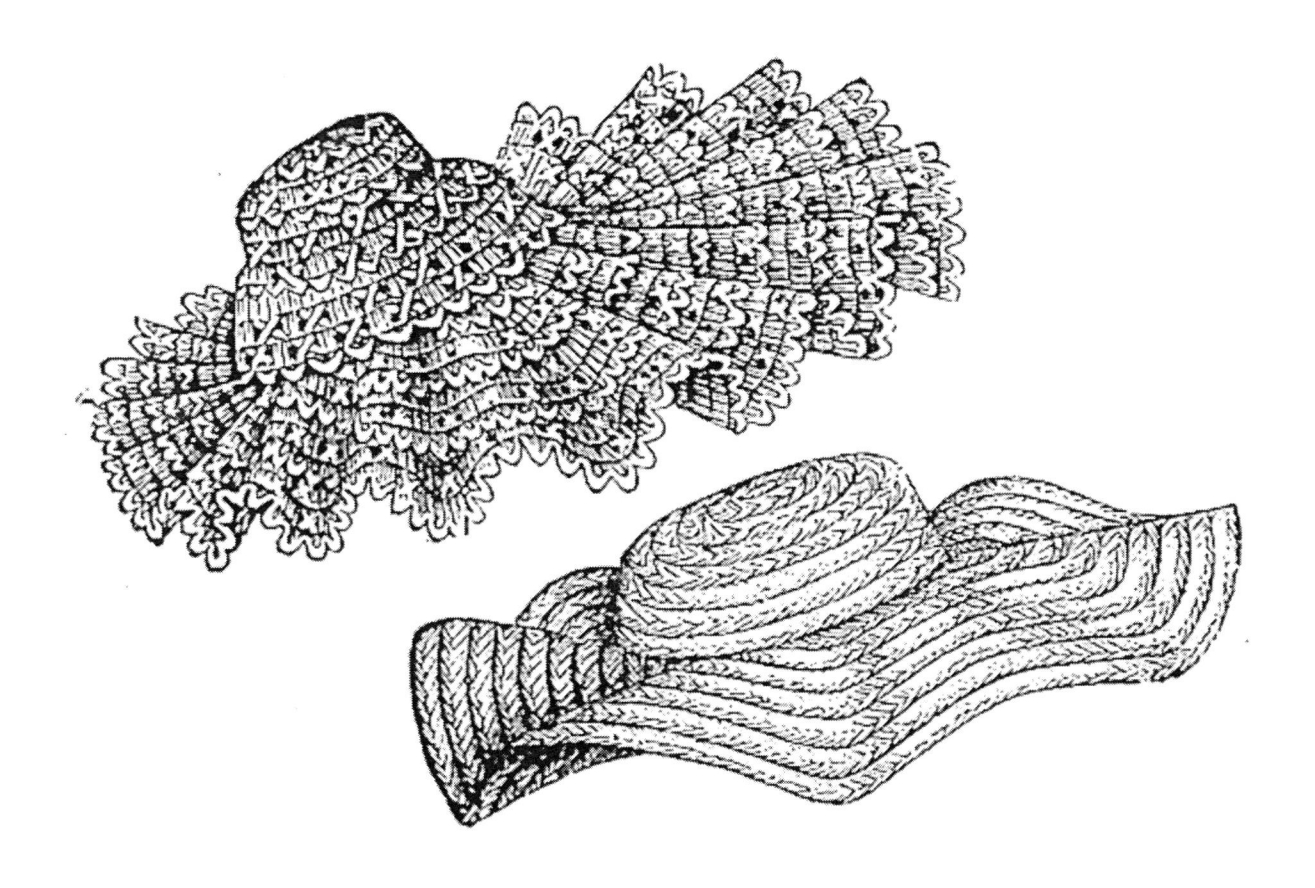

A novel hat for a girl of eight to ten or twelve years is of coarsely woven fancy straw, with a cup-shaped crown and full fluted brim. A Leghorn hat for small girls, has a crown of medium depth, and a fancifully waved and dented brim.

March 25, 1893
GIRLS' UNTRIMMED SUMMER HATS

A hat for an older girl is of yellow fancy braid, with the brim caught up at the back. Fig. 4 is a dark blue straw, with an insertion of blue and white checkered braid in the brim.

May 6, 1893

"1830" HAT

May 6, 1893

STRAW HAT WITH RIBBON TRIMMING

August 26, 1893
MOURNING BONNETS

The bonnet is a small capote smoothly covered with English crape, and trimmed with three series of narrow folds forming points, which are wired; the third point is turned backward, and between it and the one in front a crape rosette is placed. The crape veil is thirty inches wide and a yard long, including the hem; it is taken cornerwise, with the upper corner folded as illustrated. The short strings are of crape.

August 26, 1893
MOURNING BONNETS

The bonnet has nine narrow milliners' folds around the front, and crape strings and bow. The veil, which covers the entire back behind the folds is of crape twenty-eight inches wide, and is two yards and an eighth long; it is hemmed at each end, folded lengthwise, and draped on the bonnet is illustrated.

September 9, 1893
AUTUMN HATS

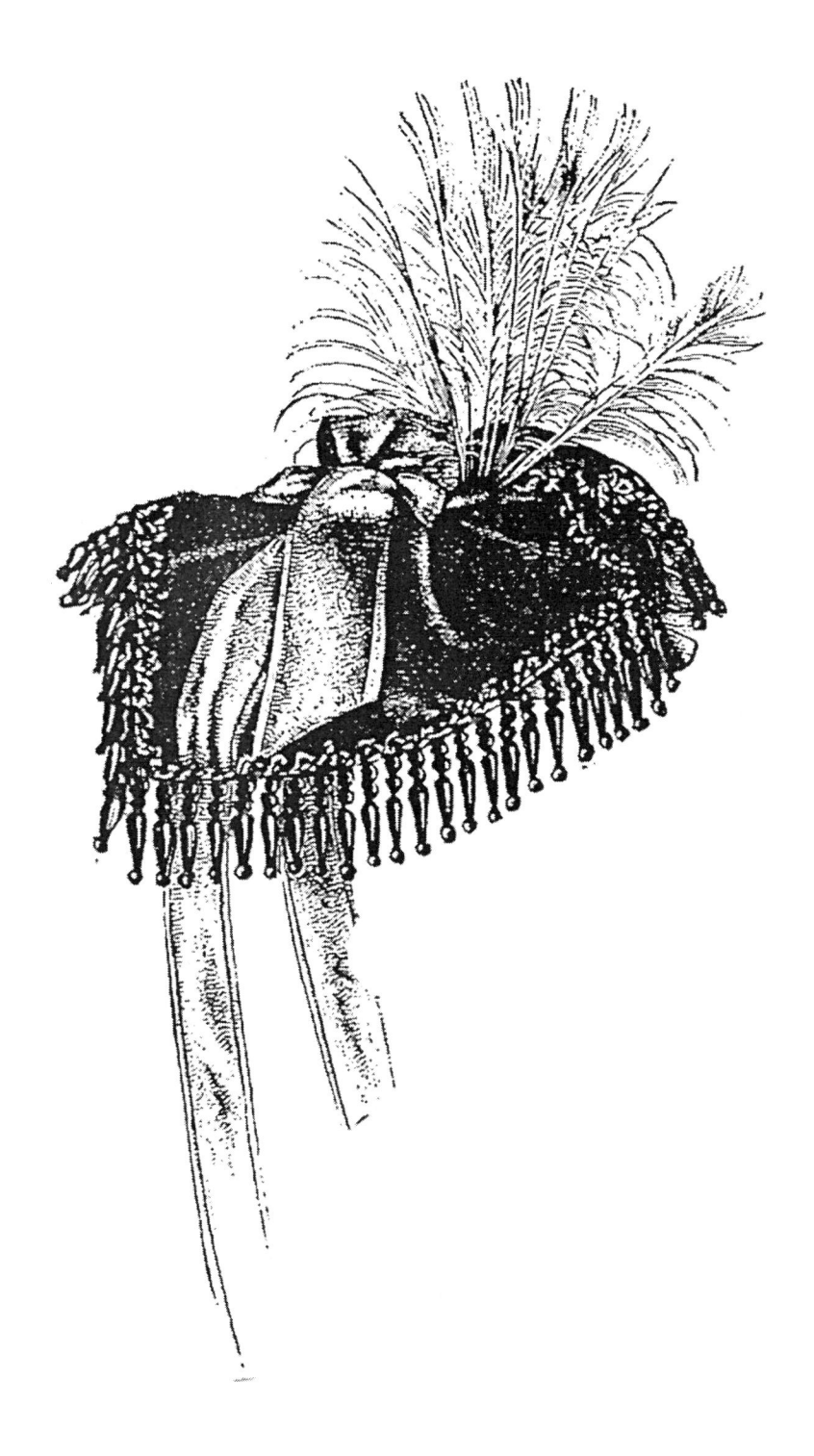

The little bonnet has a flat frame on which is draped a square of black velvet edged with jet drop fringe. The velvet is caught together in folds at the center with a bow of red velvet ribbon, to which a black aigrette is added, and the narrow strings are of red velvet ribbon.

September 9, 1893
AUTUMN HATS

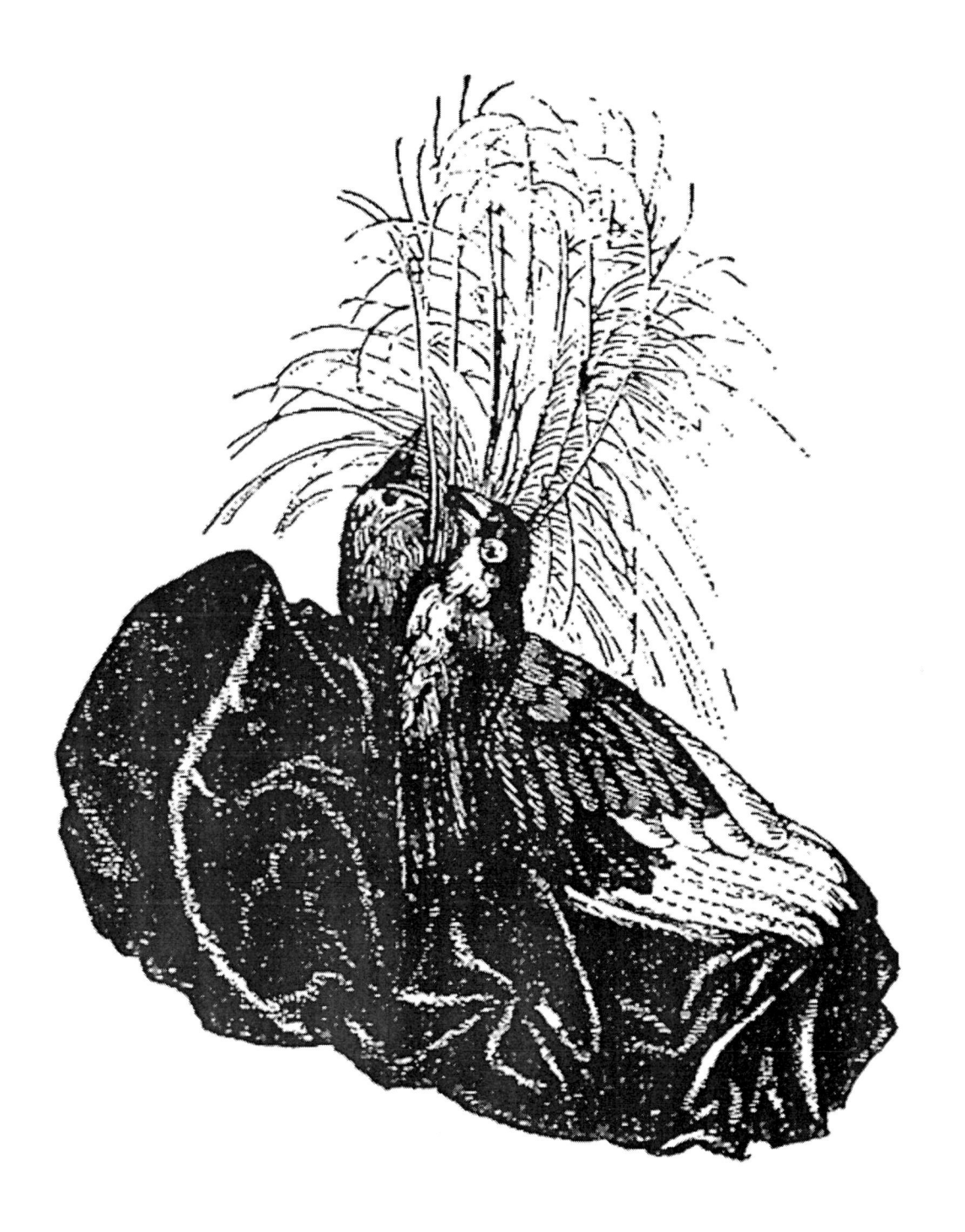

A pretty toque illustrated has a plaque of dark iridescent feathers forming the top of the crown, and dark green velvet draped about the brim. Two gray and white birds are mounted at the front, with an aigrette between them.

**September 9, 1893
AUTUMN HATS**

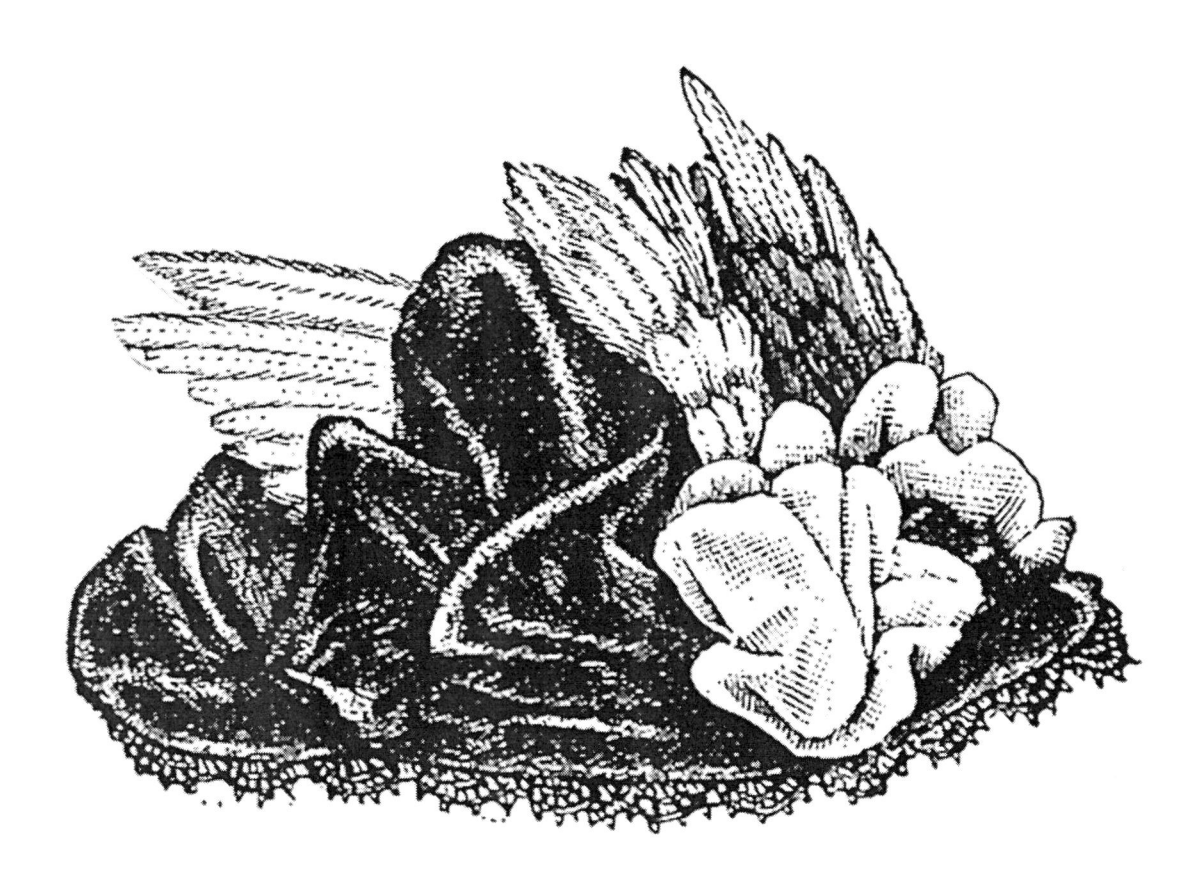

A small round hat illustrated is of a flattened shape, and covered with green velvet, which is plain on the crown and draped in puffs and folds around it. Two pale yellow chiffon *choux* are on the front, and behind them groups of brown and white wings. The brim is faced with black lace over yellow silk.

**September 9, 1893
AUTUMN HATS**

The butterfly bow illustrated, which is a favorite hat ornament, is of fine black net stiffened with wire, and studded with jet beads and spangles.

September 16, 1893
AUTUMN AND WINTER HATS

BONNET WITH JET CROWN – The bonnet has a pleated brim of green velvet, and for the crown a jet plaque terminating in leaf points which rest on the brim. The pleating is caught up on the front, and supported by four loops of black ribbon. Strings of the same ribbon are attached by small *choux* at the back. Two black ostrich tips and a thick aigrette ornament the front.

September 16, 1893
AUTUMN AND WINTER HATS

FELT HAT WITH OSTRICH TIPS – The hat is of black felt, with a brim curving to a point at the middle of the front. Black satin ribbon is twisted about the crown and arranged in an irregular bow on the front, in the knot of which three black ostrich tips are fastened. *Choux* of yellow velvet are at the sides and back.

September 16, 1893
AUTUMN AND WINTER HATS

FELT HAT WITH BUTTERFLY AIGRETTE – Is an odd little hat of light gray felt, with the brim turned up and curved in at the middle of the front and back. A tight twist of green velvet is carried around the crown, knotted at the inside of the front of the brim, and there fastened with jet pins; another knot at the back has a jet buckle. Two velvet wings are at the front, together with a feather aigrette shaped like a butterfly.

September 16, 1893
UNTRIMMED AUTUMN AND WINTER HATS

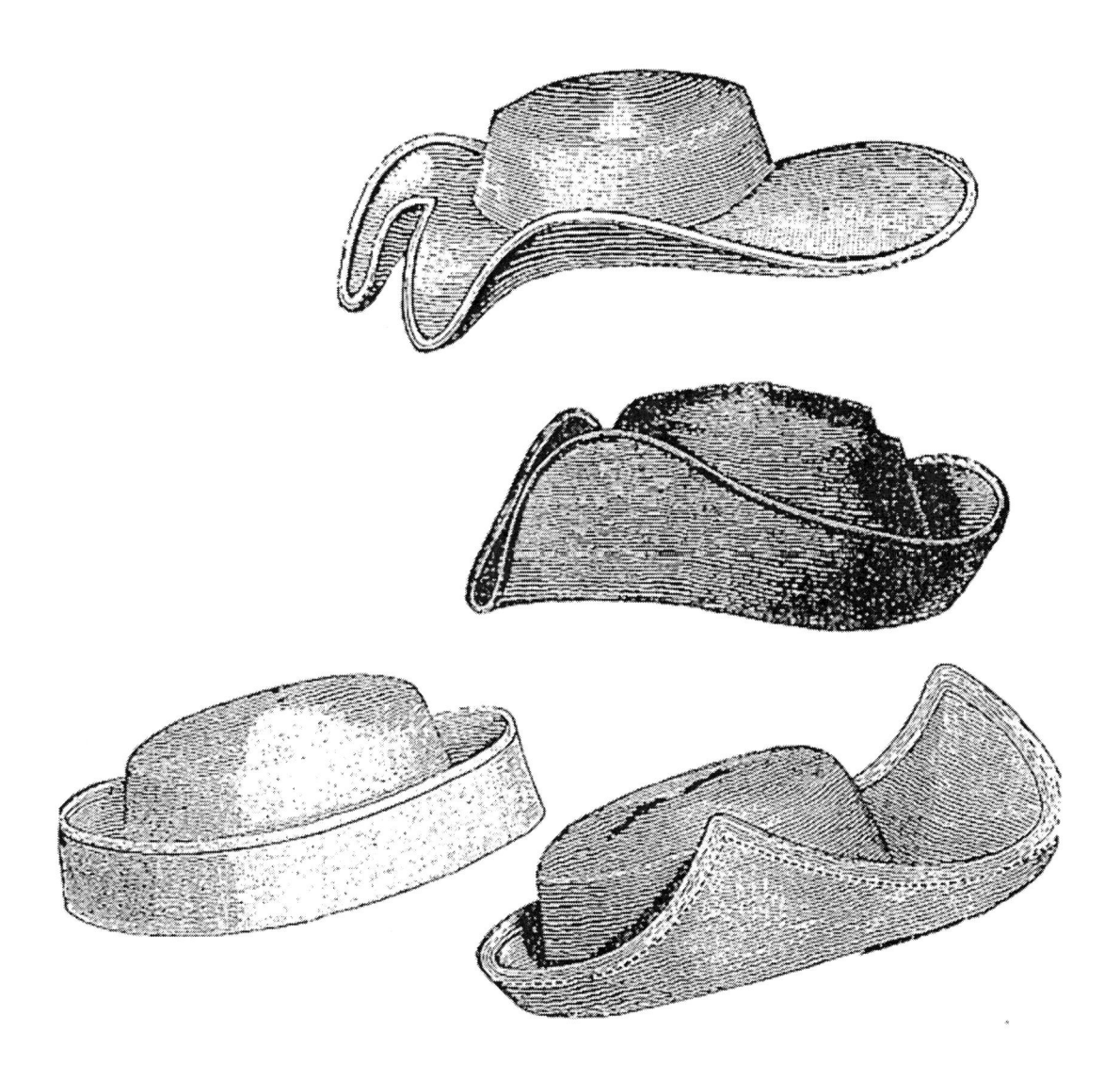

Some of the new untrimmed felts are shown. They are of moderated size, and retain the flat-topped crown, and the broad style of trimming at the front. In the group are shown a beige-colored felt with wide brim, a turned up black felt edged with silk wire, the ever-popular Spanish turban, and a hat of tobacco-brown felt, with a brim curving to a high point at the front and a lower one on the sides.

September 16, 1893
UNTRIMMED AUTUMN AND WINTER HATS

A large green felt hat in the group is edged with fur. Green and tobacco brown appear to be favorite colors in this year's felts. A bonnet in this same group is of brown felt bordered with a band of mink fur. Other felt hats shown have their brims variously reversed, slashed, and dented.

October 21, 1893
WINTER HATS

The little Stuart bonnet has a crown of dark green velvet and a reversed brim of pink and green changeable silk. At the center of the front is a green velvet rosette, from which springs a pink and green iridescent aigrette; from similar rosettes at the back wing-like points of velvet are brought toward the front. The strings are of narrow pink velvet ribbon.

October 21, 1893
WINTER HATS

The little peaked capote is of white velvet veiled with jet spangle net. The edge is fringed with a narrow white ostrich band. Two velvet rosettes, one black and one white, are placed at the front, with a pair of white ostrich tips springing from them. A similar pair of rosettes is at the back, with a black velvet loop rising from each, and narrow black velvet ribbon is used for strings.

October 21, 1893
WINTER HATS

A brown velvet bonnet illustrated has an upturned brim faced with beaver fur. A bow of brown satin ribbon is at the back, with long gilt pins thrust into it, and coming forward from it on either side is a shaded brown ostrich tip. The wide strings are of the satin ribbon of which the bow is made.

October 21, 1893
WINTER HATS

The wide-brimmed hat illustrated is of soft dark blue felt. A spangle blue aigrette is at the front, and passing in front of it and around to the back of the hat where the tip is caught to form a tuft is a shaded green ostrich plume. On the opposite side is a double twist of dark blue velvet, one end of which draws up the brim.

October 21, 1893
WINTER HATS

A smaller hat for a young girl is of dark green felt, with the rolled brim bound with green velvet. Two circular rosettes of velvet are on the front, one green and one white, with a quill thrust into each, and folds of green and white encircle the crown to cross and fasten with steel pins at the back.

October 21, 1893
WINTER HATS

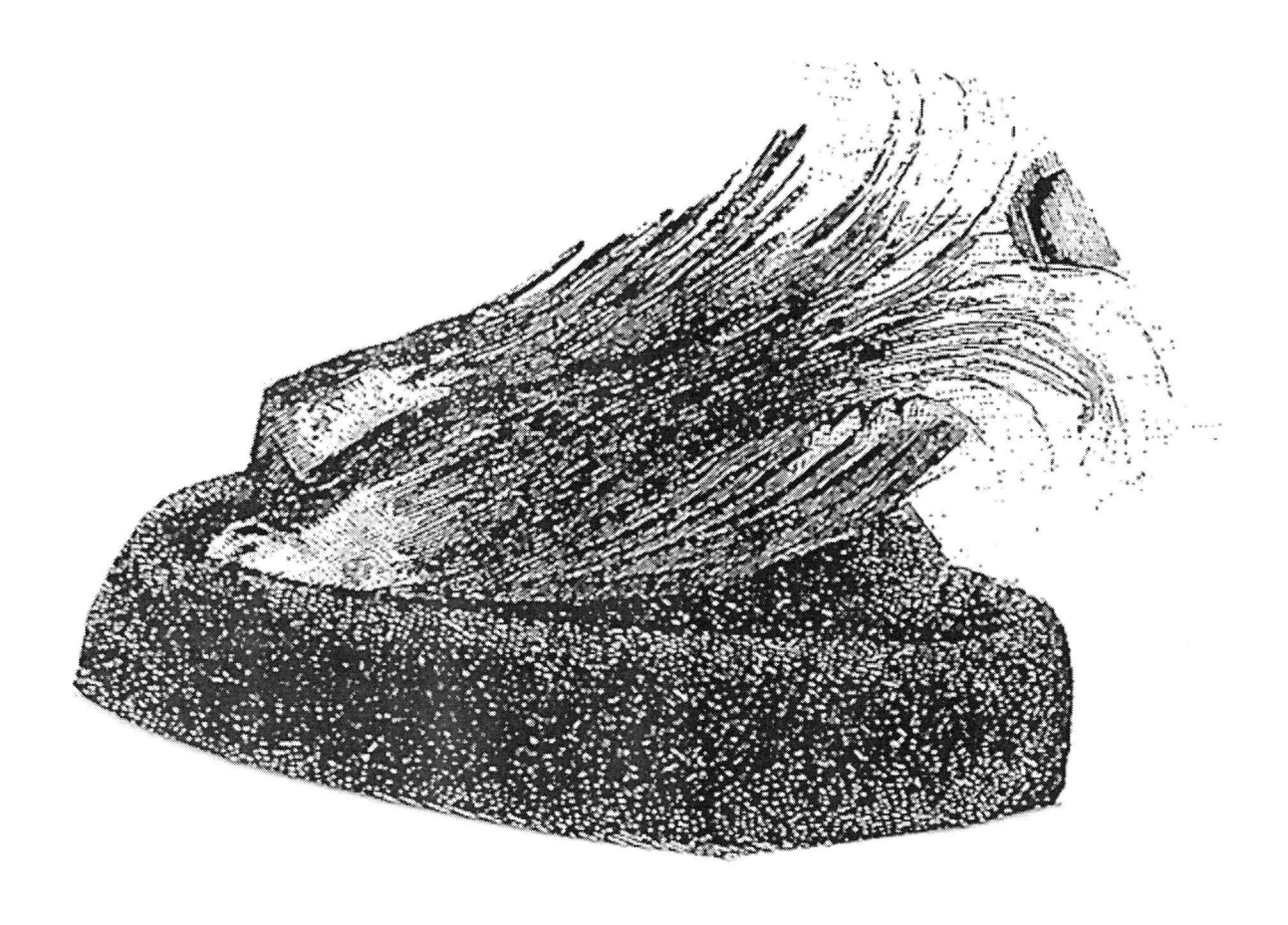

A low turban illustrated is of dark brown beaver felt, with its sole trimming a pair of shaded wings and tail feathers.

October 28, 1891
WINTER HATS

SAILOR HAT – The sailor hat has a white cloth brim bound with black, and a glazed leather crown with a narrow black ribbon band. A soft white bow and a black feather ornament are on the side.

October 28, 1891
WINTER HATS

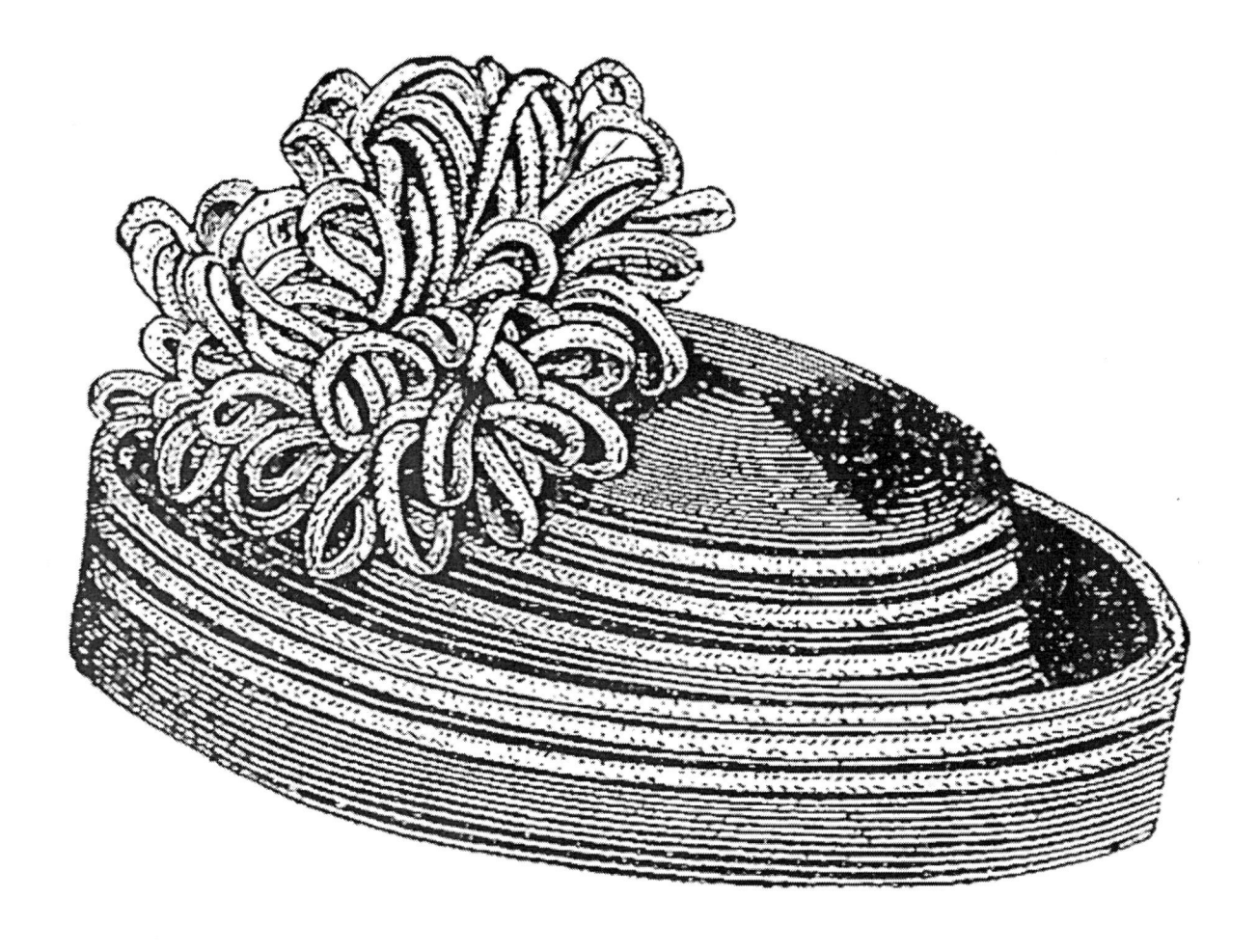

YOUNG LADY'S TURBAN – The turban is of dark blue felt. Three rows of red soutache surround the brim and crown, and a large rosette of it is at the left side of the front.

**October 28, 1893
WINTER HATS**

FEATHER TOQUE – The little feather toque has a buckram frame, which is thickly covered with white and gray pigeon feathers. An aigrette of wings is at the front.

October 28, 1893
WINTER HATS

FEATHER BONNET – The feather bonnet is in brown shades; it has a velvet facing and strings, and a bird together with a heron aigrette ornamenting the front.

**November 25, 1893
WINTER HATS**

TOQUE WITH FEATHER BRIM – The toque shown is of dark blue felt, with the brim of iridescent blue and green feathers. A scarf of spotted blue and green changeable silk is draped about the crown and twined into loops at front and back.

November 25, 1893
WINTER HATS

VELVET BONNET – The little bonnet is of dark green velvet, jetted on the crown. At either side of the waved front of the brim is placed a *chou* of black net edged with white purling, and between is a jet spangled aigrette.

April 15, 1884
YOUNG LADIES' SPRING HATS

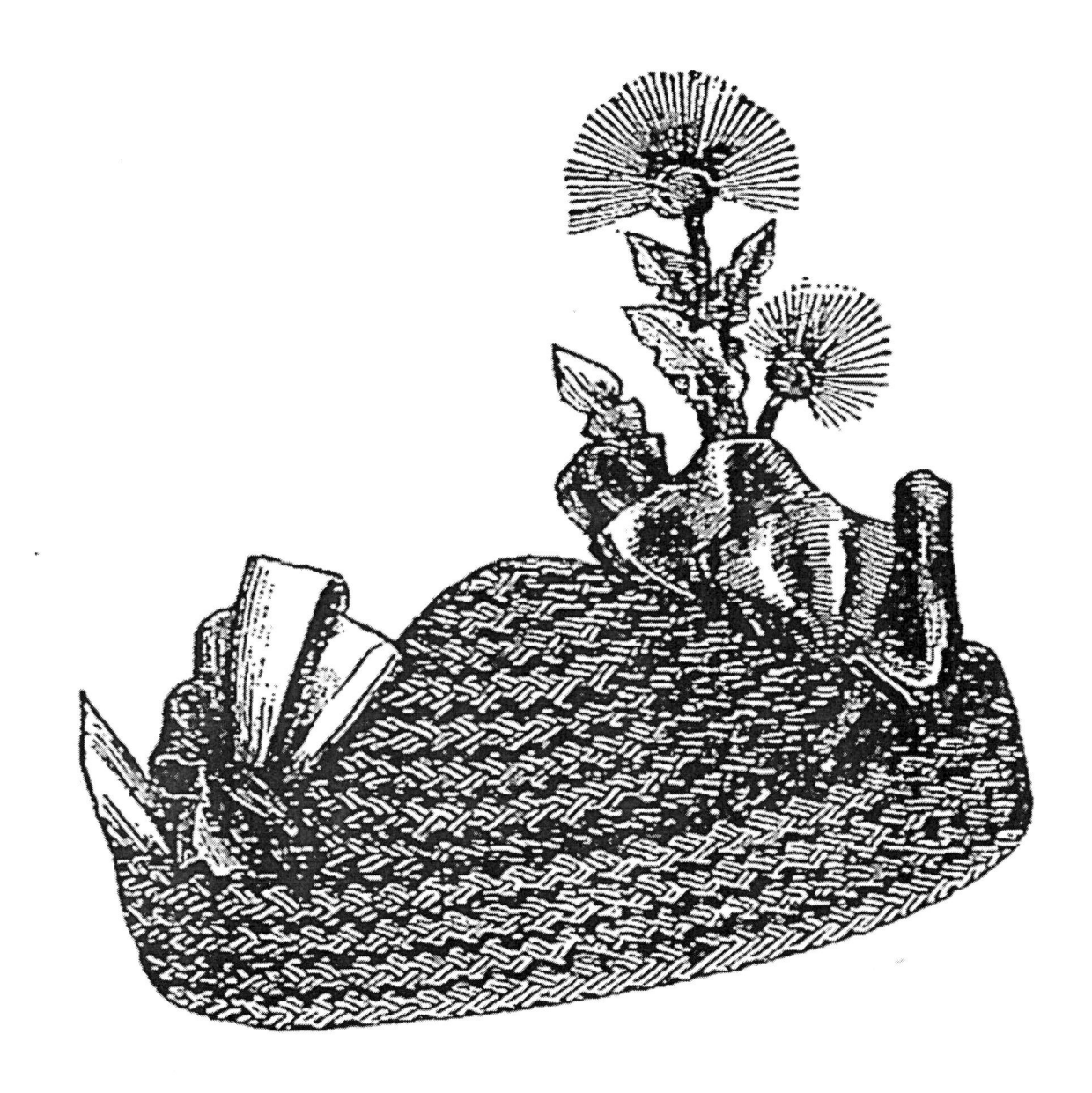

A little turban of brown rough straw, of which an illustration is given, is trimmed with double-faced brown and tan satin ribbon, which is formed into a small compact bow at the front and back. A spray of dandelion is added at the left of the front to the bow.

April 15, 1884
YOUNG LADIES' SPRING HATS

A flat-brimmed hat shown is of beige-colored straw, with the brim of notched straw in beige and brown. A scarf of brown crape is draped about the hat, studded with *choux* of brown and of pink crape, and a bunch of pink rose-buds is added at the back.

April 15, 1884
YOUNG LADIES' SPRING HATS

The crown of the hat is of light blue and brown fancy straw, with the brim of brown chip. Across the front of the hat are large *choux* of brown crape, with small ones of light blue satin ribbon between. Two blue *choux* are at the back, and a little toward the side a cluster of light blue and brown shaded ostrich tips.

May 12, 1894

THE MARQUIS HAT – The marquis hat, a charmingly picturesque model from Madame Carlier of Paris, will be worn in the summer alike by young girls and older women. Its drapery of lace softens faded complexions, and is becoming also to the youngest and those of most brilliant color. Gold-colored straw forms the hat, which is itself almost concealed by the drapery of white appliqué lace, which may be flounce or a veil found among one's treasures. The lace should be allowed to fall just below the edge all around the brim. *Choux* of faille of the color of Provence roses are set about capriciously amid the lace, and on each side of the hat is a large black aigrette springing upward from a *chou.*

June 16, 1894
SUMMER HAT

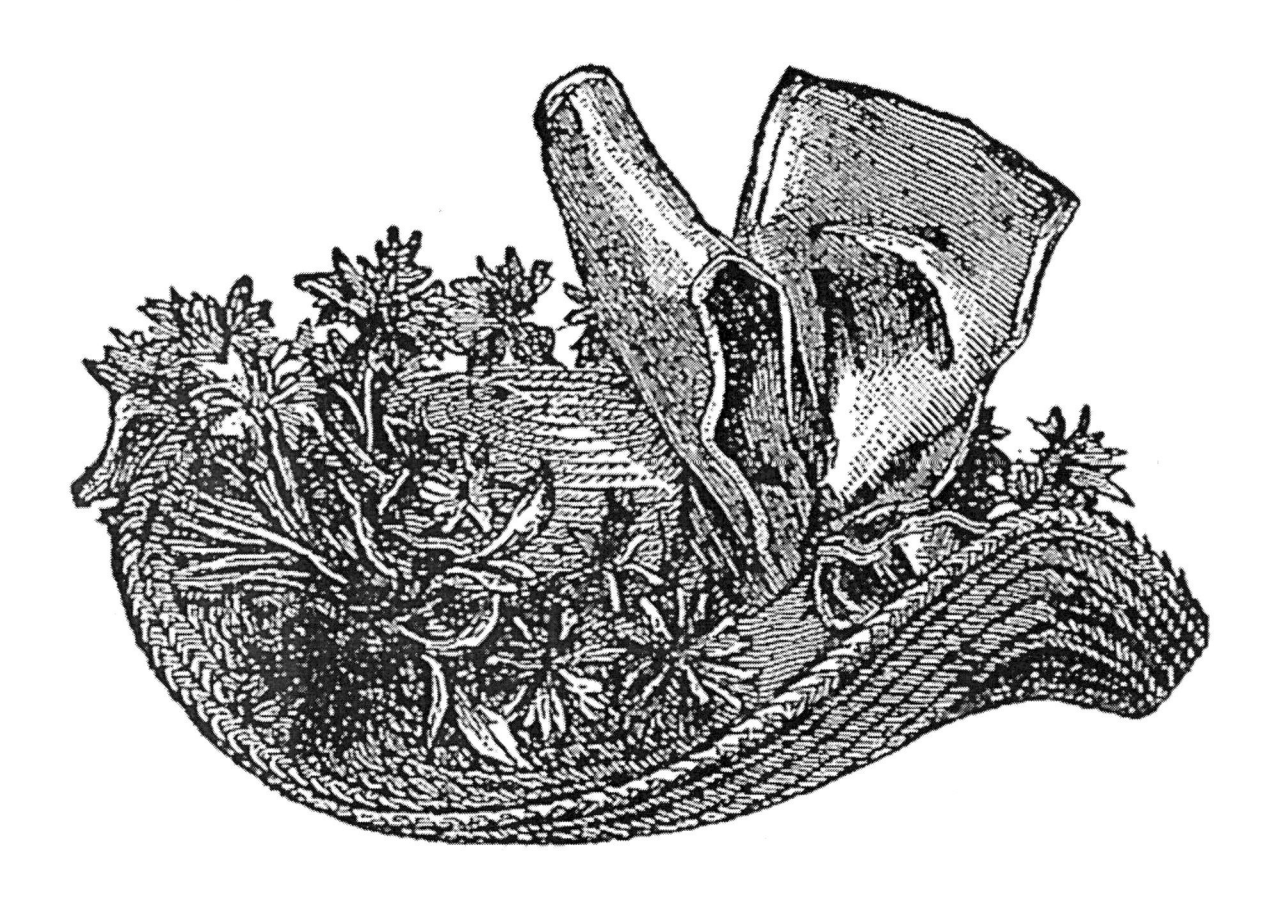

HAT WITH FLOWERS AND RIBBON – The hat has a crown of beige-colored chip with a turned-up brim of fancy straw of the same color. At the front is a large bow of four open loops of beige satin ribbon; long stemmed sprays of blue corn-flowers are on both sides, and a smaller bow of four loops is at the back.

June 16, 1894
SUMMER HATS

HAT WITH RIBBON TRIMMING – Is a hat of tobacco-brown straw with a folded band of velvet to match. A large bow of golden-yellow moiré ribbon is on the left side, composed of fan-pleatings and two high loops, and a smaller bow of the ribbon catches up the brim against the back.

June 16, 1894

SUMMER HAT – The hat illustrated is a *plateau* of pinkish mauve fancy chip, the brim of which is bent in graceful curves. A bow of wide mauve ribbon is on top of the hat, and surrounding it are sprays of shaded lilacs. Inside the hat is fitted by a black velvet band, on which, at each side of the back, are two deep pink roses.

June 23, 1894
SUMMER HATS FROM PARIS

WHITE MULL CAPELINE – A picturesque wide capeline of white silk mull is a charming summer hat for a bridesmaid, or, indeed, for any other young maiden on occasion. The model illustrated, from the Maison Nouvelle in Paris, is of lace-edged cream mull faintly tinged by a lining of palest blue silk. Rows of narrow "comet" ribbon in pale clue and cream are on the shirred mull of the brim, and a group of three *choux* of these ribbons is place at the front between the spreading loops of a white ribbon bow.

June 23, 1894
SUMMER HATS FROM PARIS

BLACK NET HAT – A shirred black net hat with an aureole brim, a model from Madame Héléna, has a soft puff of the net drooping around upon the brim. On the front a ribbon bow backed by a drapery of Chantilly lace, and rising from the center of the bow a butterfly aigrette of jet and rainbow beads.

June 23, 1894
SUMMER HATS FROM PARIS

FLOWER-TRIMMED SAILOR HAT – French milliners are decorating the sailor hat out of all semblance of the simplicity that has made of it the popular and serviceable head-covering it has so long been. First it was a single tentative *chou* of tulle or flowers; then this ornament was doubled, cropping out symmetrically on both sides of the hat; and now we have, as a further development, this model from Madame Héléna, a rush-green straw sailor, with the crown enwreathed with dog-roses, and a fan drapery of white lace rising at the back. A *voilette* or little face veil of white tulle frequently accompanies the hat.

June 23, 1894
SUMMER HATS FROM PARIS

HAT WITH LACE CROWN – White guipure lace forms the crown of a shade hat, which possesses the advantage of not crushing the front hair. The brim is of light scalloped straw, partly draped with guipure and faced with black velvet. The loops of a bow toward one side of the front are of black moiré ribbon edged with light guipure; toward the other side is a spray of pink roses with buds and foliage, and a similar spray lifts the brim at the back.

June 23, 1894
SUMMER HATS FROM PARIS

LEGHORN HAT WITH POPPIES – A white Leghorn hat from the Maison Nouvelle has a *plissé* of lace on the Empire brim. A huge bow of wide white ribbon projects forward, with folds carried toward the back, and poppies of various pink and magenta shades are thrust into every available cranny.

June 23, 1894
SUMMER HATS FROM PARIS

SUMMER HAT – A fanciful rough straw in light russet with glints of red and blue is a *plateau* which is pinched into the shape illustrated. The brim has a full facing of shot red and yellow chiffon, and is partly filled out by a ribbon bow. The ribbon is a satin-striped moiré in canary-color, banded with pale water blue. A flat Alsacian bow is on the front, with ends drawn back to form streamers, and a more voluminous bow is on the side.

June 30, 1894

BEACH HAT

June 30, 1894

SHADE HAT

July 28, 1894

MIDSUMMER HAT – The hat illustrated is for lawn parties and other summer festivities, and is designed to be worn with thin dressed of lightest muslin, crépon, or barége, and with the taffeta silks that are preferred to all silks at the present moment. Leghorn braid, or one of the golden-yellow straws, forms the wide brim curving out from the head in the flaring fashion of Empire hats. White ostrich feather tower high above the front, amid loops of yellow ribbon that surround the low crown, while another group of feathers is added low in the back. Just inside the brim a barrette or cap of loops of aubergine velvet rests on the waving hair. Strings of yellow taffeta ribbon are tied in a bow with short ends.

August 4, 1894

A BLUET HAT – This charmingly youthful hat is wholly of tulle, in the bluet-blue shade, which is the Paris fad in colors. Its large round form is made by shirring the tulle on fine wires, forming a brim, which is bordered with small double ruffles of tulle falling from a wreath of the bluets, or corn-flowers, for which the hat is named. The crown is in the shape of a large bow of tulle, and in front of it is a bow of velvet ribbon of the peculiar shade of which is in the heart of bluets. The design is from Madame Carlier of Paris, who uses with becoming effect drooping ruffles on the brim, not only of tulle, but of lace, and in black tulle as well as in colors.

August 4, 1894
SHADE HATS

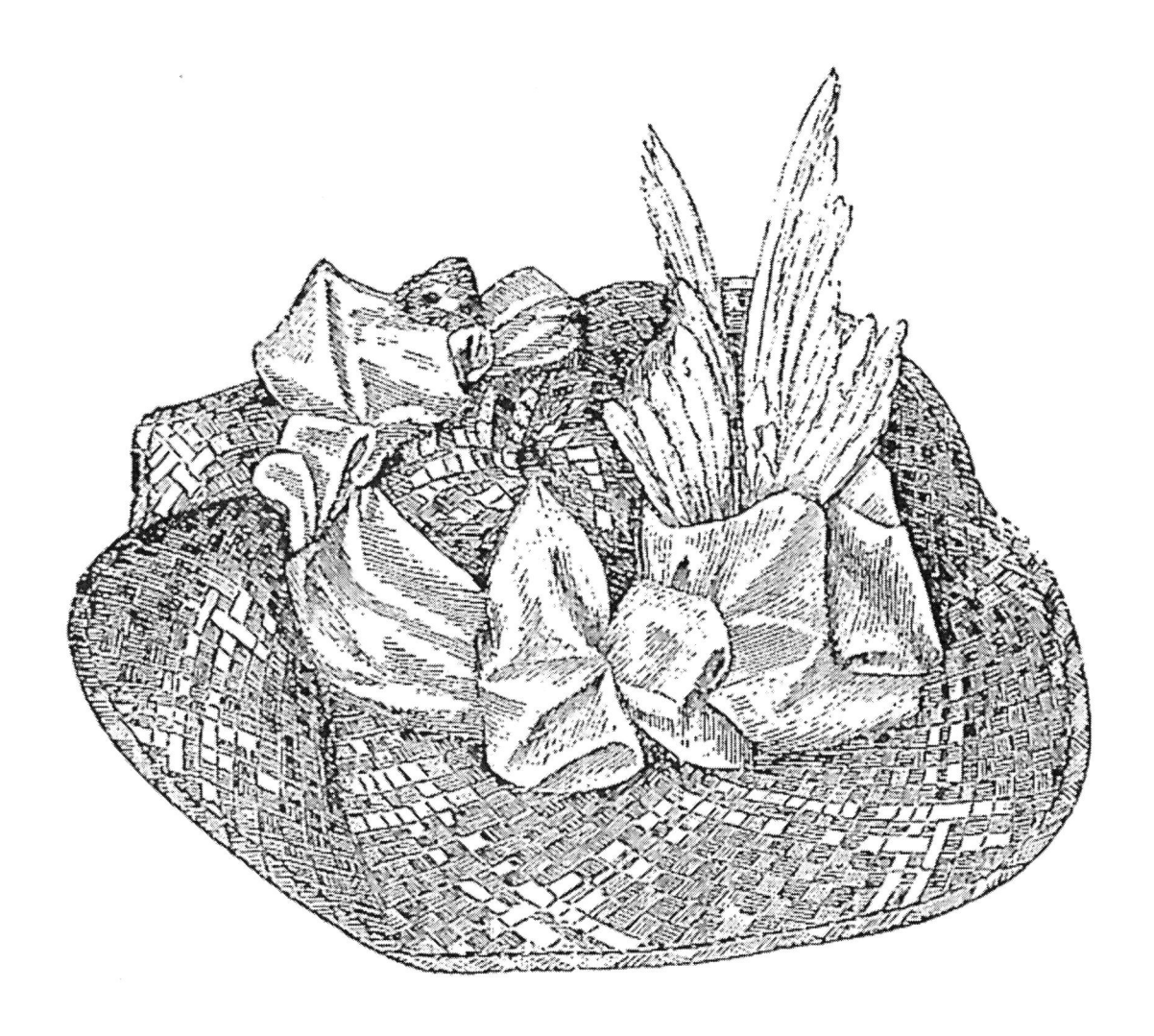

One of these country hats is of rush-green and white cross-barred straw, draped with a scarf of white China silk, which forms puffs and a bow, and toward the side a large rosette, into which a pair of white wings is thrust.

August 4, 1894
SHADE HATS

The second hat shown is of a gold-colored rough fancy plait, faced with cream silk muslin, with a pleating of the muslin projecting beneath the brim. A large bow of white satin ribbon is at the front and a smaller at the back.

**August 11, 1894
MOURNING HATS**

CRAPE ROUND HAT – A round hat covered with English crape for a young lady is a modified sailor shape. A folded crape scarf encircles the crown, and a bow is arranged at the side.

August 11, 1894
MOURNING HATS

CRAPE BONNET AND VEIL – A small capote bonnet is covered smoothly with crape and bordered with two narrow folds. Two wired loops stand up at the front, above a scarf formed into a series of short loops and ending in *choux*. The crape veil is twenty-eight inches wide and a yard and three-quarters long; it is hemmed at the ends, and draped on the bonnet at the middle of one of the long selvage sides.

August 11, 1894
MOURNING HATS

CRAPE BONNET AND VEIL – A small Fanchon bonnet of crape is bordered with alternate narrow folds and frills of crape. The veil is twenty-eight inches wide and long, and is hemmed on two sides; one corner is folded and fastened on the bonnet under an Alsacian bow of crape.

April 27, 1895
SPRING HATS

SPRING HAT – The hat is of a burnt-brown fancy straw. A knot of golden-brown velvet catches up the back of the brim, and connects by a strap to a second knot which fastens a bunch of pink and white dahlias to the crown. On the opposite side the brim is caught up with a large bow of black and white striped gauze ribbon.

April 27, 1895
SPRING HATS

YOUNG GIRL'S STRAW HAT – The hat is a light fancy braid, with a curved and dented brim. Wide taffeta ribbon in changeable tan and pink is employed for trimming, forming a wide fan-shaped arrangement caught in a *chou* at the front, while a smaller *chou* is placed in the dented back of the brim.

**April 27, 1895
SPRING HATS**

RIBBON-TRIMMED SAILOR HAT – Is a brown straw sailor for a young girl, trimmed with blue and gold changeable ribbon, mounted in a large rosette bow on either side, connected by a band across the front. Small *choux* are placed under the brim in the back.

June 29, 1895
SUMMER HATS

The graceful hat illustrated is of coarse-plait black fancy braid, having a flat-topped sloping crown and brim drooping at the sides. A broad Alsacian bow is at the front, made of wide satin-striped black gauze ribbon edged with a white straw braid. Near the back are two large white velvet roses with foliage, while catching up the back of the brim are three large pink roses.

June 29, 1895
SUMMER HATS

A very fine white Milan straw hat with broad sloping brim caught in at the back has for its sole trimming garlands and clusters of France roses true to nature in color and form, arranged with careless grace.

March 21, 1896
SPRING HATS AND TOQUES

The hat is of white rice straw. The brim is wide at the front, rolling upward slightly, and has a narrow bias binding of black velvet. A drapery of black net crosses the front, held on either side by a large irregular *chou* of green velvet, a black aigrette being added to that on the left side. A cluster of apple-blossoms is underneath the brim on the right of the back.

March 21, 1896
SPRING HATS AND TOQUES

A dressy little toque bonnet is of white mousseline de soie, with a striped pattern in jet beads and spangles. The mousseline is puffed on a small white net frame, and is carried up in a pleated aigrette on the right side, to which a cluster of black ostrich tips is added. A drapery of light violet velvet is across the front, caught with a bunch of violets at the base of the aigrette. A drapery of black net is at the back, and veils a bunch of violets placed there.

March 21, 1896
SPRING HATS AND TOQUES

Another small toque has a yellow straw crown turned up at the sides, with a diadem front of wired guipure studded with jewels. A pair of crossed jet pins is at the front, and a cluster of black tip on the left side.

March 21, 1896
SPRING HATS AND TOQUES

A light straw hat has a wide brim with a black velvet piping on the under side. A wide ecru lace is gathered and draped about the brim, with black and pink roses caught in the folds. Some high black satin ribbon loops are at the back, and underneath on the hair, a cluster of roses, a fan-pleating of lace, and a black satin bow.

April 11, 1896
SPRING HATS

A small toque hat, of which front and side views are given, has an angular crown and waved brim, and is of fancy black Neapolitan. A pleated frill of black mousseline de soie is inside the brim. A spray of pink roses with foliage is on the left side, and some fancy jet pins are placed on the right; at the back a bunch of violets on either side.

April 11, 1896
SPRING HATS

A black rough straw somewhat in English walking-hat style is trimmed with roses and ribbon in black and white. A bunch of black roses is placed on each side, with foliage between, and on the broad crown are several white roses. Flaring at the back is a large bow made of very wide ribbon, with the two colors folded into each loop so that the bow shows black from the front and white from the back.

April 11, 1896
SPRING HATS

A small bonnet made of pleated black mousseline de soie has a jet star at the center of the crown, and jet spangles at the edges of the pleating. A diadem of pinkish-violet blossoms is underneath the edge, and toward the left is a cluster of ostrich tips and an arrangement of pleated mousseline caught with a jet butterfly.

April 11, 1896

A PARIS SPRING HAT – Large hats made of the light materials, such as net, tulle, and mousseline de soie, etc., are extremely fashionable this season. The Paris hat illustrated, a model from Madame Marie Gillot, is of black mousseline de soie, trimmed on the crown with black ostrich tips, while under the brim which is turned up at the left side, is a spray of tea-roses, resting on the hair.

April 18, 1896
SUMMER HATS

A large hat of silver-gray straw is trimmed with black-edged wide gray taffeta ribbon. A large bow is on one side, and an end is carried around to a small bow opposite. At one side of the back is a full bunch of gray velvet roses with yellow centers; a smaller tuft is underneath the brim, together with a ribbon rosette.

April 18, 1896
SUMMER HATS

A more fanciful hat consists of a plateau of soft rough black straw, bent into shape. A black velvet ribbon band around the crown is caught with jet ornaments at the back and brought forward as strings. At the left four black ostrich plumes are caught with a jet star, two drooping downward and two turned up. On the right are two clusters of yellow roses, one placed outside and one inside a dent of the brim.

April 18, 1896
SUMMER HATS

A black tulle hat turned up at the sides is trimmed with wide pinkish-violet taffeta ribbon encircling the crown and forming loops and cross-pieces at the back. Pink roses shading to violet trim the left side and the back, with a standing black ostrich tip added.

May 16, 1896
SUMMER HATS

An English walking hat of dark blue straw has a sloping crown almost covered by a bias blue velvet band, and broad brim slightly raised on the sides. A broad moiré ribbon in shot blue and green is draped about the brim, and arranged in a bow on the side, to which a large bunch of ragged-sailors is added.

May 16, 1896
SUMMER HATS

A hat of gold-colored fancy straw, with flat-brimmed front and waved back, is trimmed with plissé white chiffon arrange in fans and rosettes. At the left of the back is a cluster of white ostrich plumes and a spray of pink roses.

May 16, 1896
SUMMER HATS

A white rough straw for a young lady has a trimming of five-inch flowered taffeta ribbon, which is carried in loops around the front of the crown, and raised in a high bow at the back.

July 4, 1896
SUMMER HATS

YOUNG LADY'S HAT – A simple midsummer hat for a young lady is of green straw. A white tulle scarf is draped about the crown and rises in fluffy loops at the back. A wreath and tufts of pink anemones are added to the tulle.

July 4, 1896
SUMMER HATS

SUMMER HAT – This hat of pinkish-violet straw, has three puffs of white chiffon around it, separated by twisted ribbons in shot violet and white. On the left side is a pair of white ostrich tips caught with a knot of ribbon.

July 4, 1896
SUMMER HATS

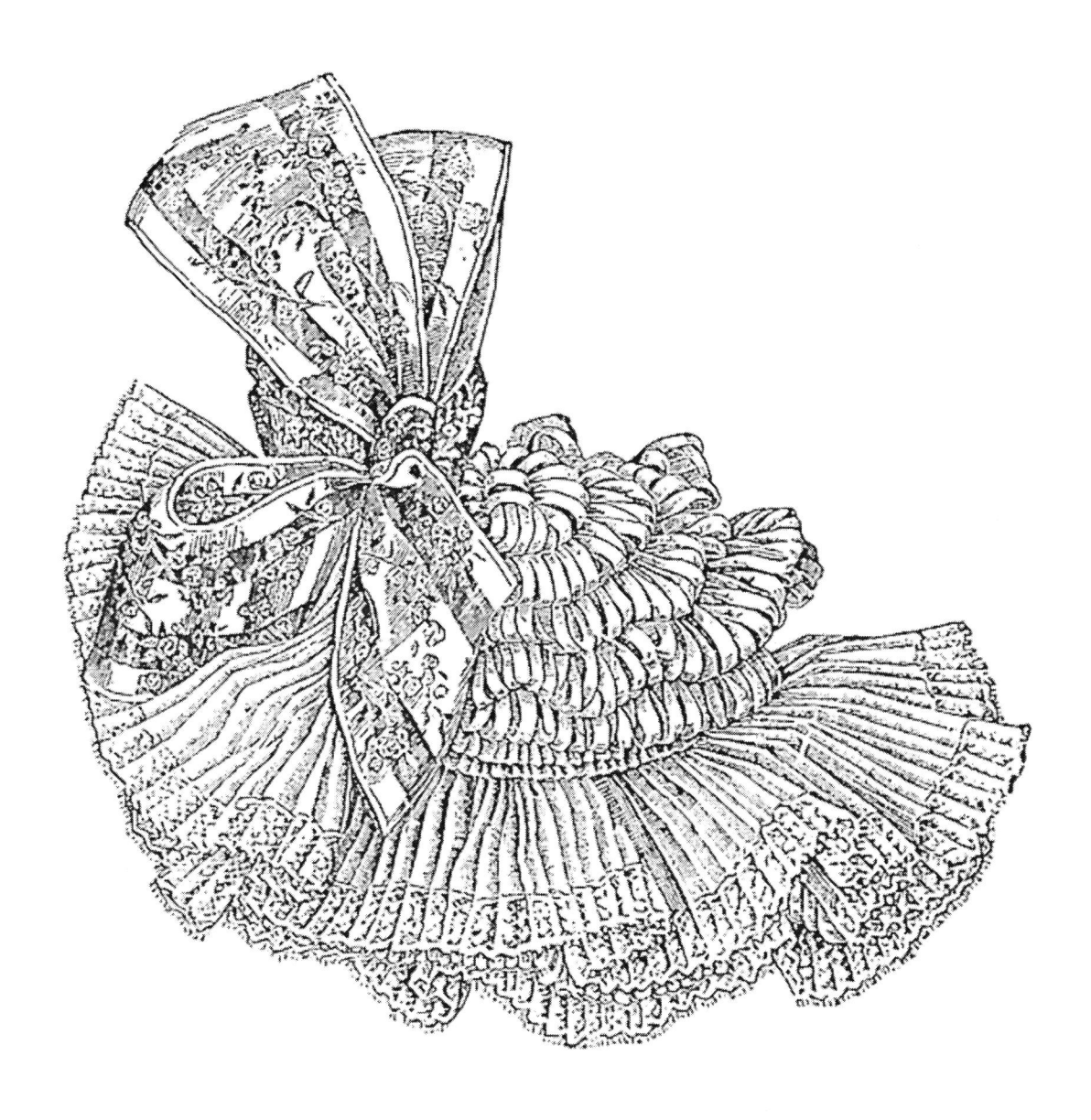

WHITE CHIFFON SHADE HAT – A picturesque shade hat has the crown of golden-yellow looped fancy straw and the brim of white chiffon shirred on wires. A pleated frill of lace-edged chiffon is inside and outside the brim. At the back is a large bow of yellow and white stripe chine-figured ribbon.

July 4, 1896
SUMMER HATS

RUSTIC BEACH OR GARDEN HAT – A simpler shade hat for rustic wear is a low-crowned sundown of light straw, with a ruffle of white lace around the edge, drooping beyond to shade the eyes, and headed by a straw cord. A puff of the lace is on top of the crown, with straw cord heading and loops.

September 26, 1896
AUTUMN HATS

The little toque hat shown is of violet velvet, made with a soft crown and a wavy flaring brim with three indentations at the front, in each of which is a large black and yellow rose. The outside trimming consists of a large black satin rosette bow hold a black aigrette and yellow bird-of-paradise feathers.

**September 26, 1896
AUTUMN HATS**

A gray felt round hat has a box-pleated ruche of gray velvet around the crown, a cluster of gray tips near the back, and some pink velvet roses underneath the brim.

October 31, 1896
WINTER HATS

FELT HAT WITH OSTRICH PLUMES – A light beige felt hat of the Amazon type is narrowly bound with black velvet and has a black velvet crown band. A large bunch of black ostrich plumes is caught with a white ribbon rosette against the side, with one drooping over the back, and another white rosette is against the upturned side of the brim.

October 31, 1896
WINTER HATS

YOUNG LADY'S HAT – A young lady's hat of glossy black beaver is faced with black satin inside the brim and trimmed with a broche ribbon in black, white, and rose, with two ostrich tips, one white and one black, thrust into the knot on the side.

October 31, 1896
WINTER HATS

HAT FOR GIRL FROM 12 TO 14 YEARS OLD – For a young girl in her teens is a stiff round-brimmed hat with the oval Russian crown that is wider than long, of dark blue felt, with a plain band and small side bow of blue and white figured ribbon, into which three slender quills are thrust, two white and one blue.

**October 31, 1896
WINTER HATS**

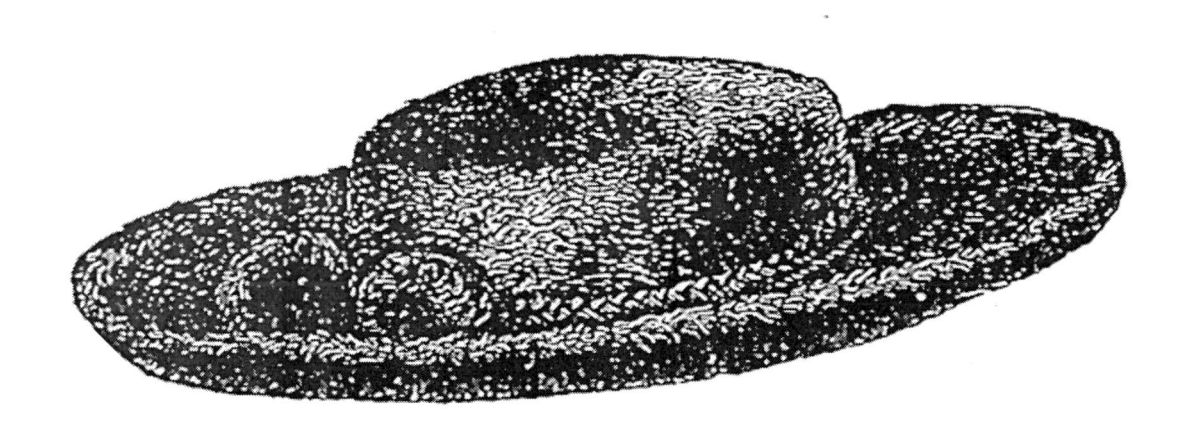

HAT FOR GIRL FROM 7 TO 8 YEARS OLD – For a small child is a rolled-brim sailor of bottle-green beaver felt, very simply finished with a silk cord and pompons.

February 20, 1897

PARIS HAT FROM VIROT – The velvet toques worn with fur capes are exceedingly soft and graceful in effect this season. In violet velvet is a particularly pretty one, made with soft brim turned up at the left side, and under the brim a bunch of Parma violets with leaves. Three long black ostrich tips in fan shape are on the left side of the crown.

**February 20, 1897
SPRING HATS**

A spring turban illustrated is of grayish-green straw, with a binding of dark green velvet. The trimming is of green shot taffeta, which forms a full scarf and high side bow with a brass buckle, and some shaded cocks' plumes are added.

February 20, 1897
SPRING HATS

An English walking hat of tobacco-brown straw has a narrow binding and three crown bands of dark olive velvet. At the side is a bunch of pink blossoms with a stiff erect bow of the velvet, and a smaller tuft of blossoms is under the brim.

April 24, 1897
LADY'S AND GIRL'S SUMMER HATS

The Alpine hat illustrated is of a light beige-colored Neapolitan braid, with the under side of the brim faced with dark green straw. The trimming is of dark green ribbon, which forms a flat crown band and side loops with a rosette.

April 24, 1897
LADY'S AND GIRL'S SUMMER HATS

A young girl's sailor is of tobacco-brown rough straw, with crown band and side bow of white grosgrain ribbon, and added to the latter a knot of brown velvet and two brown quills.

April 24, 1897
LADY'S AND GIRL'S SUMMER HATS

A hat for a child of seven to eight years is of white rough straw, with a bias frill of doubled white silk at the edge and extending as a facing in the brim. A puff of the silk is on the crown, caught with knots of white satin ribbon.

May 1, 1897
PARIS SPRING HATS FROM MADAME VIROT

A French picture hat of pearl-gray tulle has the halo brim covered with the tulle in closely shirred headings having a fluffy effect. Against the front, inside and outside of the brim, are knots of black velvet connected by a strap, the one against the brim holding a black ostrich pompon, that on the crown clasping two gray ostrich tips.

May 1, 1897
PARIS SPRING HATS FROM MADAME VIROT

A flat-brimmed sailor shape of red straw with black velvet folds has a fluffy ruffle of red mousseline de soie veiled by dotted black mousseline draping the crown. At the side is a knotted arrangement of straw and mousseline supporting a black aigrette and an ostrich plume. Mousseline *choux* are underneath the back.

May 1, 1897

PARIS HAT – A black straw hat from Carleir has a pink velvet drapery about the high crown veiled by black guipure. Black mousseline de soie *choux* hold a pair of black ostrich plumes, and bunches of pink poppies are above and beneath the brim.

May 1, 1897

PARIS HAT – A light straw hat from Marescot has a double brim, the outer part deeply waved, with a pleating of cream mousseline de soie filling the crevices. The trimming, which is placed squarely on the crown, is composed of variegated light and dark roses held by black velvet ribbon knots.

May 1, 1897

SUMMER HAT

May 1, 1897

SUMMER HAT

May 15, 1897
SUMMER HATS

Hat of Nile-green silk net, with narrow bands of green-white straw round brim; crown of silk net, with double frill of dark green silk, large bunches of sweet-William, shading from pale yellow-green to green-black, on right side, and crescent of black cut jet on left.

May 15, 1897
SUMMER HATS

The hat is entirely of black spangles, front and right side being covered with black Spanish lace. Four large tips are on the left side, and a full bow of salmon-colored ribbon finishes it at the back.

May 15, 1897
SUMMER HATS

The hat is of coarse fawn-colored satin straw; crown of cerise, velvet, and pink silk ribbon. Cream, pink, and purple roses are scattered loosely over the brim.

May 15, 1897
SUMMER HATS

The hat is of gold net, studded with jet nail-heads. Bands of gold net surround the crown, edged with frills of white chiffon. Five large tips and a black paradise aigrette are on the left side, and a cerise ribbon at the back.

May 20, 1897

NEW FASHIONS IN VEILS

Every season brings some new fashions in veiling, and also in arrangement of the veils on the hats and over the face, and this year there seem to be many new little points that are worthy of consideration.
The first point, and an eminently satisfactory one, is that there is an uncommon number of new designs in the cheap qualities of veiling, and the mesh is delightfully fine

and the threads soft, while the dots are well arranged. For as little as twenty-five cents a yard (single width, of course) an extremely pretty veil, either dotted or fancy plain mesh, can be bought. The fancy plain mesh is a great relief to the eyes after the constant wearing of the dotted; but the mesh must not be too thick, otherwise a very ugly effect is given to the skin. Neither must it be too sheer, nor, again, of too elaborate a pattern;
so it will be seen that care and taste must be exercised in the selection. At most of the large establishments mirrors are put on the counter, so the customer can try on a veil before purchasing it. In the expensive veilings the mesh is quite elaborate, and the dots are either large and far apart or small and so close together as to quite obscure the vision.

These veils, as a rule, are in double width,

and of silk instead of thread. They are consequently softer, and, it must be admitted, wear better. Double veiling has again made its appearance. This is composed of an inner veil of tulle, generally white, with another one of black with chenille dots. It has been the fad for the last two or three summers at the watering-places to wear two veils, consequently this double veiling was put upon the market.

Plain dotted chiffon veils in blue or brown or black are worn over the fancy veiling; this of course protects the skin most effectually, but it is almost too blinding for most eyes, especially if worn over small hats, for then the veiling is so very close to the face. All black veiling is more worn than any other; but white with black dots is not unfashionable for smart occasions when worn with light hats and bonnets.

There is no doubt but that may of the fashions of the first years of Victoria's reign are to be revived, and the sprigged veils then in style will be among this summer's novelties. Most exquisite is the workmanship of some of these veils which have been lain away for years, and which are now brought forward from the treasure house. They will be worn with big hats, and will hang in loose folds.

Made veils are exhibited among the new fashions. These are finished with a narrow ruffle, or the hem is trimmed with two or three rows of narrow satin or velvet ribbon;
Excepting for the net veils bordered with crépon which are worn for mourning, made veils are never so popular as the veiling by the yard, which can much more easily be arranged to be becoming. Double-width veiling is, as a rule, wide enough to allow of being cut in two lengths. It is always much more expensive in proportion that the single width, but is
to be had in much better qualities and more choice of designs – from a yard to a yard and a quarter is the length to buy.

Veils this spring are arranged to reach just to cover the chin, and the fullness is very carefully drawn up, and pinned at the back of the hat with an ornamental pin. It is necessary with almost all of the veils to put a box-pleat or gathering-string in the front at the brim of the hat, so as to prevent drawing
too tightly across the nose.

The subject of mourning veils is a difficult one to treat. Every season some new ideas are set forth as to lightening mourning. For instance, a heavily crêpe-trimmed gown and crêpe bonnet were exhibited at the recent doll show, and the veil, which hung in long folds, was of coarse net trimmed with rows of black ribbon. The effect was incongruous, for the long veils are only suitable for deep mourning. Then they should be of silk, nuns' veiling, or crêpe. In the first six month or year of wearing deep black the long veil is always worn, but not necessarily over the face, for now it is more the custom to have a face veil with a deep crêpe back. When the veil is quite short and the mourning is lightened materially, net veils trimmed with crêpe are sometimes worn. With a round hat, the face veil bordered with crêpe, or the plain black grenadine or chiffon, is the correct thing. Long crêpe veils are never worn with hats, but are reserved exclusively for bonnets, as are also silk and nuns' veiling.

May 29, 1897

TOQUE OF FANCY BLACK STRAW HAT – There is no distinctive shape in millinery this season, but all shapes are made with reference to what is becoming. In black straw is one peculiarly odd style, exceedingly soft in outline. The trimming consists of bows of mousseline de soie of two shades of red, and shaded roses of these colors, with aigrette of leaves.

June 12, 1897
SUMMER HATS

WIDE BRIMMED HAT WITH OSTRICH PLUMES – Hats this season are apparently chosen with reference to the side effect as swell as the full face. In black straw is one of which the side-lines are particularly good. The brim is slightly tilted at the left, and shows underneath some soft ostrich tips. Around the crown is a double pleated frill of stiff pink taffeta starting from a narrow black velvet band, which is finished in front with a long-looped bow-knot and small steel buckle. A tuft of black ostrich plumes is put on most gracefully at the left side.

**June 12, 1897
SUMMER HATS**

HAT TRIMMED WITH WINGS AND PLISSÉS – Another black straw hat trimmed with pink taffeta is effective at the side. This hat has a broad band of black velvet around the crown, with three pleatings of pink taffeta put on in rosettes. Stiff black wings are put in between the rosettes in an odd but smart effect.

June 19, 1897
SUMMER HATS

LOUIS XVI HAT – Hats are no longer simple shapes of straw, but are composed of several different materials. In shirred pink tulle is one favorite style with brim at the back turned up sharp and square, the space at the back of the head filled in with black velvet ribbon tied in a Louis XVI bow-knot, the loops and notched ends stiffly wired. A broad rhinestone buckle fastens the velvet bows. The entire front of the hat is covered by a very large shaded pink silk poppy.

**June 19, 1897
SUMMER HATS**

SHIRRED TULLE HAT – Another odd hat has a curved brim turned up at the back, and is covered with several bias folds of pink taffeta, and with a fancy straw braid finishing the edge. At the left side of it is a spray of roses and a cluster of violets. Bunches of violets are also at the back, under the brim.

**June 26, 1897
SUMMER HATS**

SUMMER HAT WITH ROSES AND QUILLS – A burnt-yellow straw hat, slightly raised at the back, has a wreath of roses and foliage around the crown and a bunch of black quills on the side.

June 26, 1897
SUMMER HATS

HAT TRIMMED WITH POPPIES – A hat trimmed with scarlet poppies is of Manila-colored straw, with a waved brim faced with red straw underneath. A large bow of red ribbon veiled with black net is toward the side at the front, and starting from the bow a wreath of poppies goes around the crown, while clusters of the flowers are under the brim.

**June 26, 1897
SHADE HATS**

Of the two shade hats shown, one is of white straw, with a full pleating and puff of white mull at the edge. Around the crown is a band of black velvet, and over it white gauze ribbon, which is arranged in a bow on the left. The other hat is in black straw and mousseline de soie, the crown and part of the brim being of straw, the outer part of the brim of shirred and wired mousseline covered with pleatings. A red satin ribbon bow is toward the front.

July 10, 1897
SUMMER HATS

A wide-brimmed *capeline* of fancy Neapolitan, the brim of which curves becomingly over the face, is trimmed with white and green shot taffeta ribbon and a cluster of drooping white plumes held in a rhinestone buckle. Flowers are clustered against the back of the brim.

July 10, 1897
SUMMER HATS

A gray straw English walking hat has a broche ribbon crown band, and on the side a cluster of in-curving gray ostrich tips held by a steel buckle.

July 10, 1897
SUMMER HATS

A wide-brimmed light straw has on the crown a flaring windmill bow of violet velvet holding some pansies and a cluster of shaded plumes.

July 10, 1897
SUMMER HATS

Soft and becoming in effect is a sailor shape with the crown and the bird upon it enveloped in white chiffon drapery.

July 10, 1897
SUMMER HATS

A wide straw with a Tam top to the brown of lace over green silk, and green velvet folds around the crown, has a side cluster of feathers held by a buckle and a lace jabot.

July 24, 1897

The hat shown is one of the favorite red straws of the season. Double pleatings of white and red gauze project at the top of the crown from black velvet band, some loops and black feather pompons are on the side, and underneath the back a bunch of red and white poppies.

September 18, 1897
FASHIONABLE HATS FOR EARLY AUTUMN WEAR

A large cream-colored Leghorn has the crown trimmed with tiny frills of narrow yellow Valenciennes lace, and the brim draped with white tulle which fastens three long white plumes.

September 18, 1897
FASHIONABLE HATS FOR EARLY AUTUMN WEAR

A walking hat of rough white straw is trimmed with stiff white wings, in front a bow of white taffeta, and has long black plumes on either side. Under the brim at the back are rosettes of white taffeta.

September 18, 1897
FASHIONABLE HATS FOR EARLY AUTUMN WEAR

Another rough white straw hat is turned up at the left side to show a bunch of green roses. On the top of the hat are soft white ostrich tips with a high stiff bow of white taffeta, which gives height and a smart look. A wide white tie, with the ends tied in front in bow-knot, is worn with this hat.

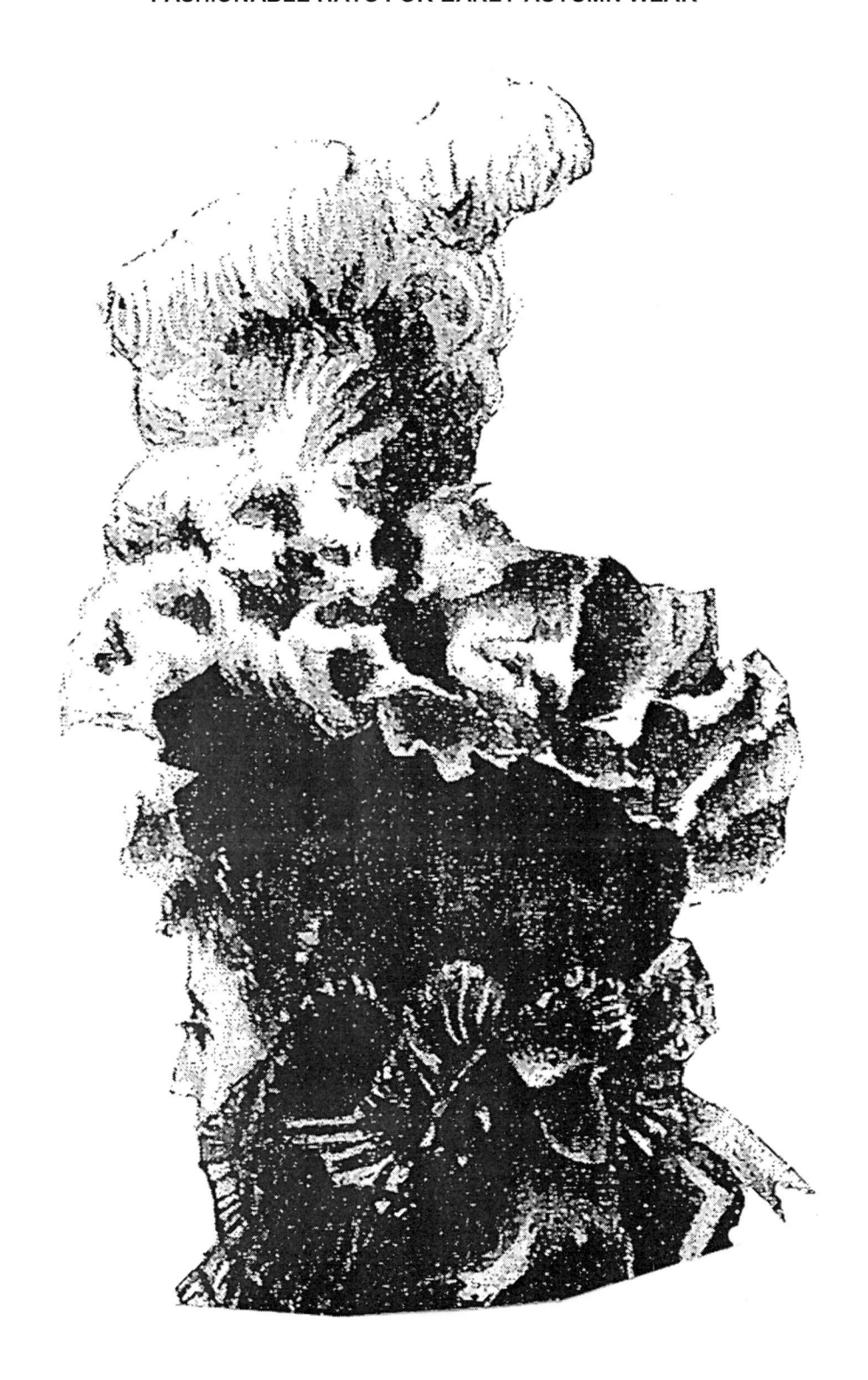

September 18, 1897
FASHIONABLE HATS FOR EARLY AUTUMN WEAR

In mousseline de soie and yellow lace is a smart hat, with crown of straw, and odd effect of black velvet *cache-peigne* and band around the crown. A cluster of white tips is placed at the left of the crown.

September 18, 1897
FASHIONABLE HATS FOR EARLY AUTUMN WEAR

Purple straw draped with white lace is another combination, made more effective by a cluster of big purple silk flowers. The brim is flat and edged with white lace. A broad bow of purple taffeta ribbon stands up in front, while the ends cover the crown. At the left side is a high spray of big purple silk flowers with buds.

September 18, 1897
FASHIONABLE HATS FOR EARLY AUTUMN WEAR

A rough silvery straw trimmed with purple taffeta bow and bunches of clover is exceedingly smart and quite novel in design. The brim is covered with pleated taffeta ribbon and edged with velvet. Bunches of shaded clover are around the crown and under the brim at the back, while wide bows of taffeta ribbon give breadth and height.

September 25, 1897
AUTUMN HATS

A graceful autumn hat is in silver gray relieved by a touch of clear reddish-violet. The under side of the brim is faced with gray velvet, while outside the entire hat is draped with gray moiré antique, which forms irregular puffs and folds and curves over the edge of the brim. Above the raised left side is a cluster of ostrich tips, of which four are in silver gray and one in violet, while against the under side of the brim is a knot of violet satin ribbon.

**September 25, 1897
AUTUMN HATS**

A golden-brown felt hat with flat brim and medium high crown has two long plumes of a lighter shade of brown curling about the crown, the stems held by a knot of darker brown velvet ribbon.

September 25, 1897
AUTUMN HATS

The feather ornament illustrated, composed of a pair of wings and an aigrette, is in gray tones shading to white.

November 13, 1897
HATS FOR THE HORSE SHOW

A bonnet of blue-black velvet is embroidered in silver-gray silk and cut steel. A frill of duchesse point-lace is put around the front and sides, and finished at the back in a butterfly bow. At the left side are graceful pompons of white marabout feathers, fastened with long pins of Roman pearls and brilliants. Narrow black velvet strings are fastened at the back of the bonnet and are tied under the chin.

November 13, 1897
HATS FOR THE HORSE SHOW

A large hat of castor velvet has the brim faced with white velvet. The trimming consists of two long plumes the same color as the velvet, most gracefully adjusted. A silver and rhinestone buckle fastens the feathers to the hat.

November 13, 1897
HATS FOR THE HORSE SHOW

The poke bonnet is revived again, with most graceful modifications and much more trimming than was in fashion on the poke bonnets of olden time. In black velvet is a smart model which has the brim edged with a ruche of black mousseline de soie. Around the crown and extending down on the hair at the back is a boa of white feathers. Just at the back is a white dove together with a long sweeping black aigrette perched on a cluster of black satin antique poppies.

November 13, 1897
HATS FOR THE HORSE SHOW

Extremely odd, but none the less effective, is a toque of dove-gray chiffon, which forms a foundation for a covering net-work of chenille fastened with small rhinestones. At the left side is a high arrangement of white shirred satin antique and white marabout feathers. At the back is a large pin of amethysts and rhinestones.

November 13, 1897
HATS FOR THE HORSE SHOW

A picture-hat, which is most elaborate in construction but has graceful lines, is of black velvet. It is trimmed with large black ostrich plumes. The crown is nearly hidden under loops of black taffeta ribbon, and the ostrich plumes are fastened with bows of black taffeta and a large buckle of brilliants set in old-silver. Broad black taffeta streamers are fastened at the back of the hat, and can be worn tied under the chin or left loose at the back. These streamers are too eccentric a fashion to be recommended for general wear.

November 13, 1897
FASHIONABLE WINTER HATS FROM KNOX

A felt walking hat turned up at one side is trimmed with band and bows of black satin and a bunch of eagles' feathers.

November 13, 1897
FASHIONABLE WINTER HATS FROM KNOX

An Astrakhan brim is combined with an embroidered velvet crown, and trimmed with a cockade of white ostrich tips, making a most charming and becoming toque.

November 13, 1897
FASHIONABLE WINTER HATS FROM KNOX

In gray felt a smart walking hat is noticeable for its good lines and odd coloring. It is trimmed with an owl's head and wings.

November 13, 1897
FASHIONABLE WINTER HATS FROM KNOX

A toque of black velvet which is soft in outline has a brim of Astrakhan, and is trimmed with black ostrich tips.

November 13, 1897
FASHIONABLE WINTER HATS FROM KNOX

Gray is a favorite color this season, and a smart picture-hat is of gray velvet, with brim turned up at the left side. The trimming consists of ostrich and osprey plumes the same color as the velvet.

November 13, 1897
FASHIONABLE WINTER HATS FROM KNOX

A dark blue velvet hat worn off the face is novel from the feathers that trim it – ostrich tips of dark blue shading into white. The brim is bound with black velvet, and there are black satin bows between the tips.

November 13, 1897
FASHIONABLE WINTER HATS FROM KNOX

Essentially refined and smart is a hat of plum-colored shirred velvet with soft crown of satin antique embroidered with jet. Black ostrich feathers are adjusted so that one falls over the brim at the back.

November 13, 1897
FASHIONABLE WINTER HATS FROM KNOX

An odd toque is of black satin antique, with brim turned up at the side and fastened with a full rosette of black tulle. The crown is formed of two bands of shirred cerise velvet, and two ostrich plumes turn away from the brim over the crown.

November 13, 1897
FASHIONABLE WINTER HATS FROM KNOX

In the new shade of sapphire-blue velvet is an effective and smart toque, with black satin rosette at the left side, and two black ostrich tips, with osprey aigrette.

November 13, 1897
FASHIONABLE WINTER HATS FROM KNOX

A black velvet bonnet without strings is an odd little affair – quite small, and with brim bound with shirred velvet. A double bow of black satin ribbon and black and white ostrich tips comprise the trimming.

November 13, 1897
FASHIONABLE WINTER HATS FROM KNOX

Hats trimmed with fur and made of fur are again to be fashionable, and are, as a rule, most becoming in shape and color. In mink fur is a particularly effective toque, with a brim of shaded blue velvet showing beneath the mink. At the back of the hat mink tails are arranged to stand quite high, and are fastened with a wide and elaborate buckle of sapphires and rhinestones.

November 13, 1897
FASHIONABLE WINTER HATS FROM KNOX

A severe and somewhat trying style of walking hat is of tan, with brim faced with brown. The crown and band of trimming are of moiré velvet, and at the left side is a bunch of owls' feathers.

November 13, 1897
FASHIONABLE WINTER HATS FROM KNOX

A blue velvet straight-brim hat is quite covered with long white ostrich plumes, the only other trimming being a bow of white satin ribbon.

November 13, 1897
FASHIONABLE WINTER HATS FROM KNOX

Another style of walking hat of gray has the brim faced with black. The trimming is black moiré velvet and eagles' feathers.

November 13, 1897

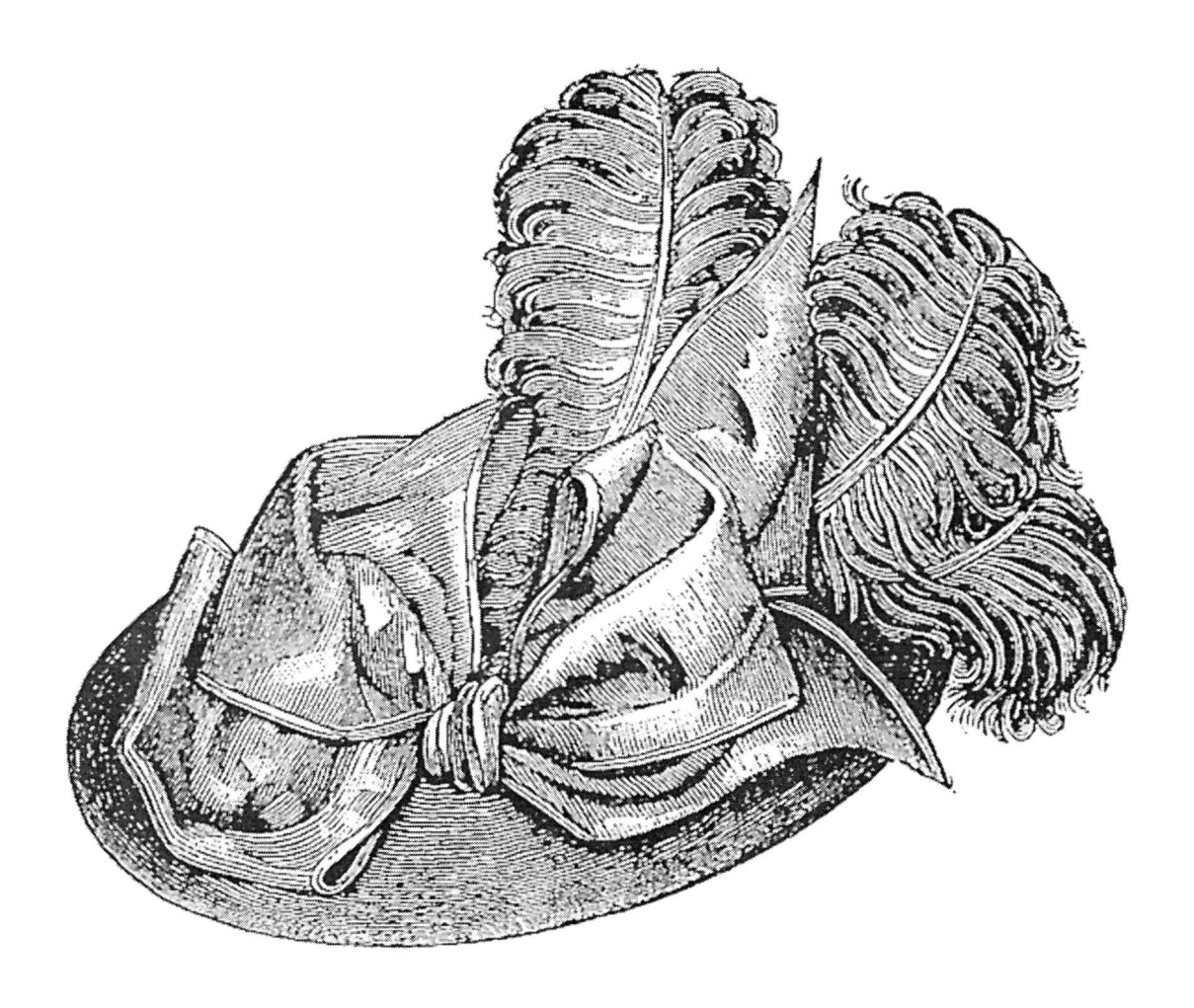

WINTER HAT

November 13, 1897

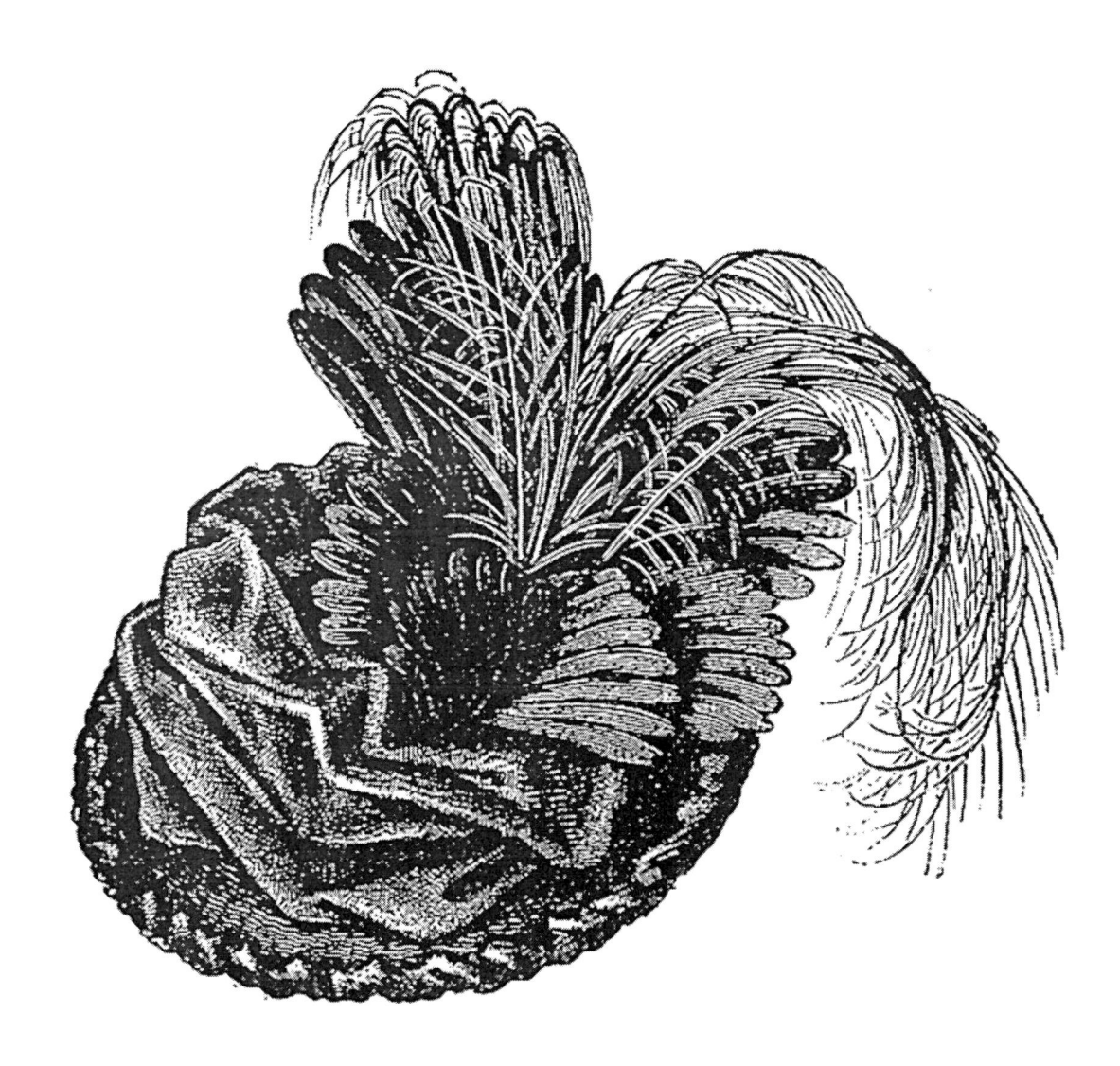

WINTER HAT

November 13, 1897

WINTER HAT

March 12, 1898
SPRING HATS FROM PARIS

HAT WITH GRAY PLUMES AND ROSES – The hat in the Louis XVI style is of straw trimmed with plumes, which are separated in front, or rather at one side of the front, by a band and knot of cerise taffeta. Under the brim at the side are silk roses of the same color as the taffeta. The color of the straw is a very deep yellow, and the feathers are of a tan shade.

March 12, 1898
SPRING HATS FROM PARIS

MODEL FROM CARLIER – Another youthful hat is made of fancy black straw, and worn quite far off the face. The brim is turned up, and in front is covered by black ostrich tips, which fall forward. On the back of the hat are more of these ostrich tips, and directly in front, apparently holding the brim up, is a rosette of cerise taffeta.

March 12, 1898
SPRING HATS FROM PARIS

HAT FROM RÉBOUX - Again the Louis XVI fashion is repeated in a most picturesque hat, larger than any of the other described. It is of green straw, and is trimmed with mousseline de soie and green taffeta. At the left side are two wood-color ostrich tips fastened with a large rhinestone buckle. This hat curves up at one side most becomingly, and is altogether very soft and dainty in coloring and effect. It is a style that is not becoming to every one, but when it is, is immensely so.

March 12, 1898
SPRING HATS FROM PARIS

TOQUE FROM RÉBOUX - A combination of white tulle and black aigrettes forms a very odd hat. The crown is of white tulle, and black aigrettes are turned back on either side from the center of the hat, where there is a big rosette of cerise taffeta. The brim, which hardly shows at all, is of straw. This rosette of cerise taffeta directly over the face would be very trying to most people were it not for the softening effect of the white tulle and black aigrettes.

March 12, 1898
SPRING HATS FROM PARIS

GREEN STRAW HAT WITH VIOLETS – A very spring-like and effective little hat is made of green taffeta and straw trimmed with bunches of violets with quantities of green leaves. The hat is worn far down over the face, and the straw gives the effect of two crowns. The violets are massed over the crown of the hat and at the back, and the leaves and bows of taffeta stand up quite high. The coloring is most dainty and artistic. The hat itself is rather small; but then most hats this season are small, or seem so when put on top of the massive coiffure which is so much the fashion.

March 12, 1898
SPRING HATS FROM PARIS

BONNET OF BLACK OSTRICH FEATHERS – A small toque is apparently composed entirely of black ostrich tips, which are so arranged that they droop towards the face, not backward, while at the back of the tips is a large blue taffeta rosette fastened down by a jeweled buckle. In front there is no color to be seen at all. This is a very pretty style of toque, and one that will surely be very fashionable on this side of the water, as it is becoming both to the profile and the full face.

March 26, 1898
SPRING HATS

A dainty rose toque is composed entirely of large open roses shaded in pink. The sole trimming is a black velvet bow with high wired loops placed at the middle of the front and caught with a rhinestone ornament.

March 26, 1898
SPRING HATS

Another small hat, which, like the toque, is worn quite far back, is of black tulle spangled. The entire crown is spangled. The brim is covered with shirred plain tulle with a ruche at the edge. Against the front are large *choux* of turquoise-blue chiffon holding a cluster of jetted quills.

March 26, 1898
SPRING HATS

A white rice-straw summer hat is in a small high-crowned sailor shape. A scarf of light green chiffon is draped loosely around the crown and entwined with pink roses and foliage. On the left side is a bunch of roses and some small blossoms, and roses are placed underneath the brim.

August 27, 1898
MOURNING HATS

A widow's bonnet illustrated is a small close capote shape, smoothly covered with crape, with two rolled folds at the front heading a narrow white ruche. The crape veil draped upon it is made of a width of forty-inch-wide crape, sixty inches long, with a deep hem at the bottom.

August 27, 1898
MOURNING HATS

A round hat for a young lady, somewhat in turban shape, is smoothly covered with crape, with a narrow fold at the edge. A double puff of crape goes around the crown, and a large bow of crape loops and pointed ends is on the left.

August 27, 1898
MOURNING HATS

A lighter hat for second mourning has a soft toque crown of crinkled black mousseline de soie, surrounded by frills of the black and of white chiffon edged with narrow ruches, and is finished with a standing bow on the up-turned left side.

December 2, 1899

Soft felt toque made of red velvet, and with brim trimmed with fur. At the left side are bows of velvet and two ostrich tips made to curl over the top of the hat.

December 2, 1899

Tan felt hat with stiff brim, trimmed with soft silk bows of the same shade of coloring. The hat is made to wear down over the face.

December 16, 1899

Picture-hat of black satin and velvet, trimmed with black ostrich feathers. Large satin rosette on the front of the hat.

December 16, 1899

Walking hat of black panne velvet with shirred brim of chiffon, and fold of chiffon around the crown. At the back of the hat are two soft bows of figured velvet.

DIRECTIONS FOR MAKING BONNET FRAMES AND BONNETS
May 9, 1868

WITH the aid of the accompanying figures, our readers will be enabled to make their own bonnet frames, cheaply and easily, which will often prove a great convenience to those living in the country. We also give the patterns of the latest styles of bonnets, which it is often difficult or impossible to obtain in small places.

The making of a bonnet frame is very simple; the material needed is foundation muslin, coarse and fine wire, and, for some styles, some silk.
    For the simple forms, shape first the outer edge of the frame of coarse wire, allowing the ends to lap over about an inch, and fastening them together as shown by Figs. 1 and 2, with fine wire such as is used in making flowers. Instead of this, fine bonnet wire may be used, which is easily taken out. The so formed wire circle (see Fig. 1), the size of which is according to the size and form of the frame, and is designated in the descriptions accompanying each, must now be bent into the requisite form as shown in the pattern accompanying each description. The ends of which are fastened together must always come in the middle of the back of the frame. The cross wires, of fine wire, must next be fastened to this, as shown in the patterns and accompanying descriptions. Each of these pieces should be cut about half an inch longer than is given in the cut. The ends of these cross wires are wound around the outer edge of the frame work as shown in Fig. 4. It is well to use scissors or a knife in order to make the fastening firm. The points where the wire crosses are fastened by means of threads, the ends of which are tied. Having finished the frame work, stretch the foundation muslin lightly over it, fastening only on the outer border.
    For the frame of a black bonnet use black foundation and black wire, and for a white bonnet white material; for a lace or crape bonnet in colors wind the frame with narrow bias strips of the same material, and cover the foundation with several thicknesses of the same, in order that it may not show through. Pliers are used for cutting the wire; if these are not at hand make an oblique cut with the scissors, after which it is easily broken. The most simple style here given is the "Metternich" Fig. 5 (see page 14). In making the frame for this, fashion the outer part of the framework from a wire twenty-five inches long, after the pattern given, as shown in the illustration Fig. 1. The cross wires are placed as shown in the accompanying illustrations Figs. 2-8. Over the prepared framework stretch tightly a piece of foundation, hem-stitch it over the outer wire, cut the edges away a quarter of an inch from the edge of the wire, and sew this down on the inside of the frame. Fig. 7 (see page 14) is the Marie Antoinette. Begin this by fastening the ends of a wire twenty-four inches long in the manner shown by Fig. 2, bend it in the shape given by the pattern, and fasten to this the middle long wire and the cross wires as shown by Figs. 3 and 4. On this lay the doubled stuff bias along the middle line, and cut the sides, leaving half an inch of the material beyond the edge. In the front part lay the pleat as shown above and sew the foundation to the outer wire. The Augusta bonnet (see page 13) is made after the same pattern as the Marie Antoinette.
    The "Pompadour" bonnet, Fig. 6 (see page 13), consists of three bands and a headpiece of the foundation muslin. In forming this, cut first of any silk at hand – it is immaterial whether it be old or new – two bias bandeaux, each two and a half inches wide, the one eleven and the other twelve inches in length; in addition to these a straight piece of foundation muslin twelve and a half inches long, for the front band. The material of the bandeaux is to be laid over on both sides at the distance of three-fourths of an inch from the edge, so that each finished band shall be one inch wide. In each of the seams made by thus folding the material lay a fine wire and back stitch if fast. The upper edge of the stuff may be laid under in a narrow hem and then hemmed to the under edge as shown by fig. 8. In order to give the silk bands the shape as per the pattern pieces, the outer side of the stuff must be stretched and the wire bent as shown in the pattern. The finished bandeaux are fastened together at the points designated by the numbers. Then cut according to the pattern piece, a piece of foundation muslin, bias along the middle, and extending a quarter

of an inch beyond the edges. This must be sewed to the bands on the under side, holding the material in as required be between the number 56 and 57. The Pompadour and Watteau (see page 14) are made in this manner.

Having completed the frame, proceed to cover it with the material chosen. The manner of doing this, as also the arrangement of bows, flowers, lace, feathers, etc., can scarcely be described, but must be learned from illustration, and will depend on individual taste and the skill of the maker. It only remains to mention that the material must always be put on bias, so that it can be stretched at will, whether it be plain, pleated, or puffer over the frame. In putting on the outside material – if it be plain it must be tightly stretched – lay it over the frame, cut it at the distance of half an inch beyond the edge of the bonnet, and sew it fast to the foundation on the inner side, taking care not to let the stitches be visible on the outside. Line with tulle or material like the bonnet.

The borders may be made in different ways. Take either a piece of the bonnet material, or, in case that be light, of silk or velvet of the same color. Figs. 9-11 show a rounded border. Take a bias strip two inches wide, as shown by Fig. 9, and sew it on the bonnet, taking care to sew through the double material, and to draw the thread tight; lay the stuff over the edge and hem down on the under side so that the stitches shall not show on the outside. The border shown by Fig. 12 is made in a similar manner, but in this a fold without a cord is laid on the right side. This may be of a different color from the bonnet.

Still another border is made by a bias strip of stuff one and a half inches in width; lay the edges over at the width of a quarter of an inch (see Fig. 13), fold the strip together at half its width, and fasten one end to a corner of the bonnet, laying it so that the middle seam made by doubling shall lie exactly on the front edge of the bonnet; stretch the strip along the edge till it exactly fits, then fasten it on the other corner and hem down on the inside. On the outside the border will lie smooth, and does not need to be fastened.

For the band simulating a diadem, which is seen on the front of may bonnets, sew together two widths of bonnet wire, each nine inches long, and cover them with a strip of bias material, five inches wide, laying in a piece of stiff muslin. Fig. 14 shows a finished band. The ends must be fastened inside near the front edge of the bonnet. The remainder is left loose.

As the bonnets are mostly fastened under the chin by means of tulle or crape, the ribbons are usually narrow. They are sewed on the corners of the bonnet, and tied back under the hair. This ribbon is folded down to the width of an inch by making two pleats, and is then sewed on as shown by Fig. 17.

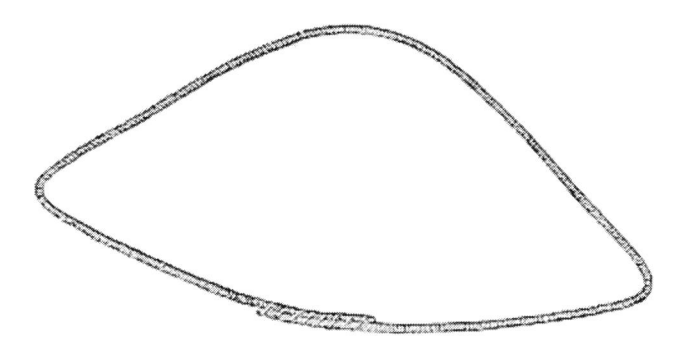

Fig. 1.—Outer Wire of Bonnet Frame—Reduced.

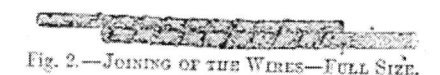

Fig. 2.—Joining of the Wires—Full Size.

DIRECTIONS FOR MAKING BONNET FRAMES AND BONNETS
May 9, 1868

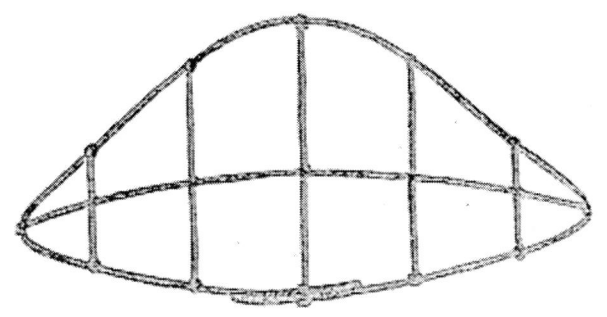

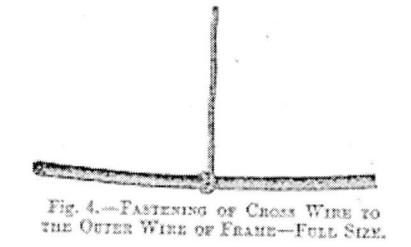

Fig. 3.—Wire of Bonnet Frame—Reduced.

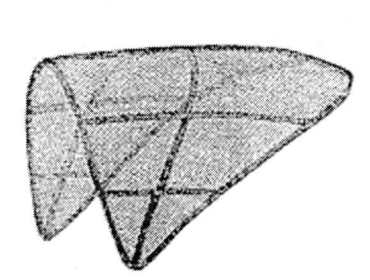

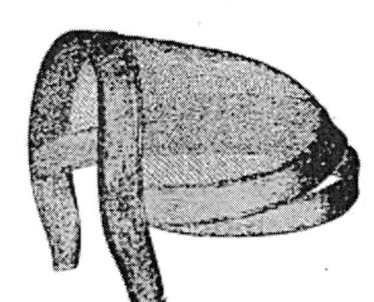

Fig. 4.—Fastening of Cross Wire to the Outer Wire of Frame—Full Size.

Fig. 5.—Frame of Fanchon.

Fig. 6.—Frame of Pompadour.

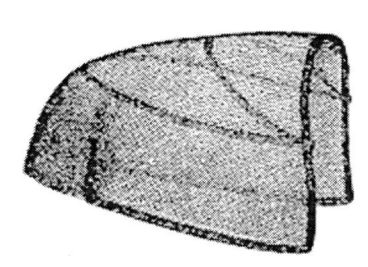

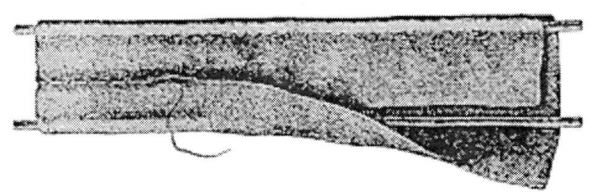

Fig. 7.—Frame of Marie Antoinette.

Fig. 8.—Manner of Making Bandeau for Pompadour—Full Size.

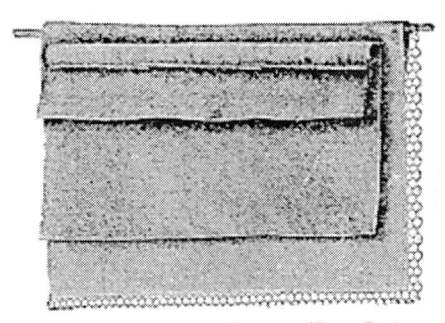

Fig. 9.—Binding of Bonnet—Full Size.

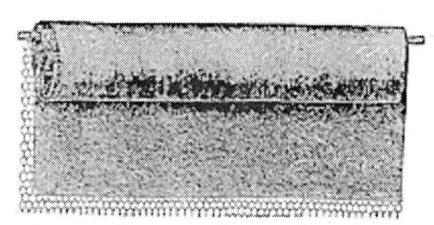

Fig. 10.—Binding of Bonnet—Full Size.

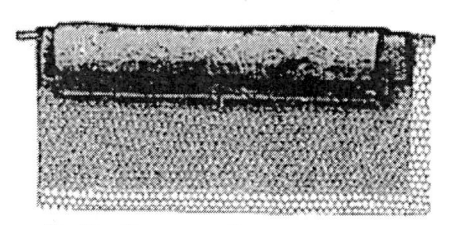

Fig. 11.—Binding of Bonnet—Full Size.

DIRECTIONS FOR MAKING BONNET FRAMES AND BONNETS
May 9, 1868

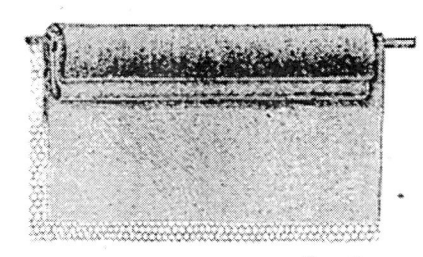

Fig. 12.—Binding of Bonnet—Full Size.

Fig. 13.—Bias Strip for Binding—Full Size.

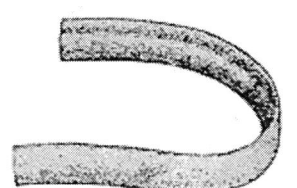

Fig. 14.—Bandeau for Bonnet—Reduced.

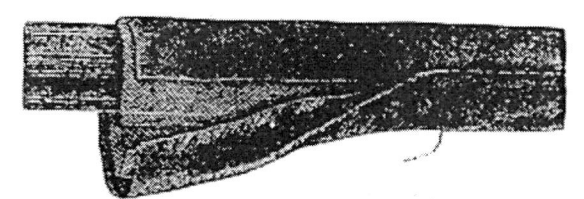

Fig. 15.—Joining Wire for Bandeau.

Fig. 16.—Manner of Making Bandeau—Full Size.

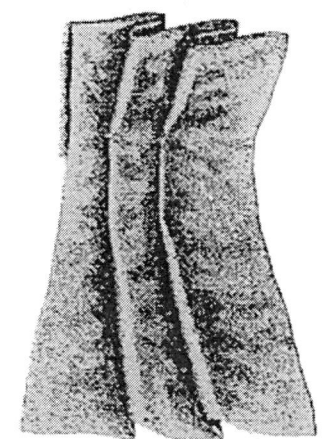

Fig. 17.—Manner of Sewing on Strings.

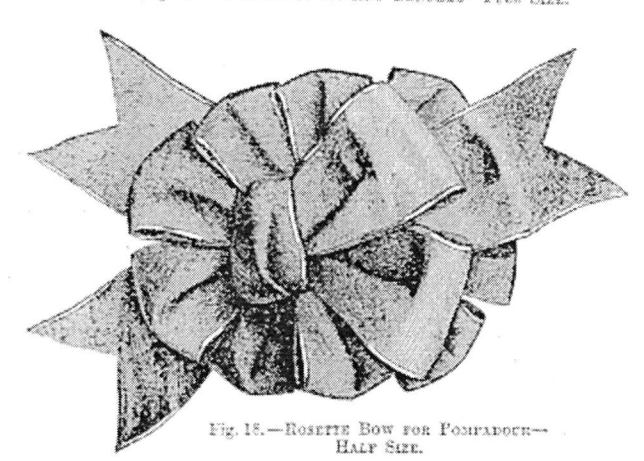

Fig. 18.—Rosette Bow for Pompadour—Half Size.

Fig. 19.—Satin Bow for Trianon—Half Size.

Fig. 20.—Fan-Shaped Bow for Metternich—Half Size.

LADIES' STRAW SAILORS

1898 SHAPES READY

Knox Hats

All Mail Orders promptly executed. Send for 1898 Catalogue.

Knox Hatter
194 Fifth Ave.
Fifth Avenue Hotel
New York

Rough Straw, $4.00   Smooth Straw, $5.00

FOR CORRECT STYLES IN

Trimmed Millinery, Wraps, Suits, etc.,

Send 15 cents for Sample Copy

RIDLEY'S FASHION MAGAZINE,

2000 ILLUSTRATIONS, with LOWEST NEW YORK PRICES affixed to each article. Address

EDW'D RIDLEY & SONS,
Grand, Allen, and Orchard Sts.,
NEW YORK.

LADIES STRAW SAILORS
1899 SHAPES NOW READY

KNOX HATS

All mail orders promptly executed. Send for 1899 Catalogue.
FIFTH AVENUE HOTEL

KNOX-HATTER 194 FIFTH AVE. N.Y.